EXPERIMENTS WITH WATER

BOOKS BY HARRY SOOTIN

Experiments in Magnetism and Electricity
Experiments with Electric Currents
Experiments with Heat
Experiments with Machines and Matter
Experiments with Magnetism
Experiments with Static Electricity
Light Experiments
The Long Search: Man Learns About Air
Science Experiments with Sound
The Young Experimenter's Workbook
Experiments with Water

EXPERIMENTS
with Water

by HARRY SOOTIN

Illustrated by Julio Granda

A W. W. Norton Book
Published by
Grosset & Dunlap, Inc., New York

CONTENTS

FOREWORD

This book offers the reader a series of experiments with water, one of the most widely distributed substances on our planet. If you follow the directions faithfully, you will, I hope, enjoy the resulting scientific experiences. However, to get the most out of this book you should read carefully, perhaps more than once, the two text pages introducing each group of experiments.

Most of the experiments, you will soon discover, relate to important principles in physics and chemistry. It is therefore not enough merely *to do*; the reader should also understand what he or she is doing. This understanding can come only from ideas, and ideas come from reading and thinking about what you observe in your experiments.

Do not regard the explanations on the text pages as providing answers to all questions that may arise. There are other books, thicker books, with longer and more detailed explanations. If you are especially interested in some of the subjects treated here, then you should proceed to read more about them. The list of books and encyclopedias in the back of the book, under the heading *Further Reading*, is for the reader who wants to learn more. Why not use this reading list? A few hints on the page listing these books will help start you off.

Finally, you will find that some of the experiments are quantitative — meaning that measurement is involved. This type of experiment presents a special challenge, and I hope the reader will rise to it. How skillful an experimenter are you? Can you work swiftly and accurately? Remember to repeat these measurement experiments until your results are fairly close to the accepted figures. Keep trying and you will improve your experimental skills.

WHAT YOU SHOULD KNOW

...about the rise of liquids in tubes

You are going to investigate the rise of liquids in tubes of various lengths. First, you will place a light-colored drinking straw in water. You will compare the level of the water inside the straw with the level of the water outside the straw. Does water pressure or does atmospheric pressure account for the level of the water inside the straw? Explain.

You will then apply your mouth to the straw and draw some of the air out of it. You will cause the water to rise about halfway up the straw and then quickly place your finger firmly against the top of the straw.

Will the water remain in the straw when you remove the straw from the container? Try it. Note that the atmospheric pressure is now pushing *directly* against the liquid at the bottom of the straw. This atmospheric pressure supports the downward pressure of the water inside the straw *plus* the pressure of the air remaining above the water inside the straw. Do you think this inside air pressure is now equal to or less than the atmospheric pressure outside? Explain.

You will punch three or four small holes in the upper part of another straw, using a pin or a needle. Try drawing water up this straw. Can you reduce the air pressure inside the pierced straw? Does this straw "work"? Explain.

You will use tape to join two straws end to end, and then do the same with three straws. You will try to make water rise in these long straws. Will the water rise in them as readily as in shorter straws? Try it and then explain what happens.

Remember that the atmospheric pressure on the water surface in the container is what pushes the water up the tube or straw. The suction created by your mouth merely reduces the air pressure inside the tube. The longer the column of water to be pushed up, the greater must be the reduction in air pressure within the tube. Why does it take more effort on your part to make water rise to the top of a long tube than to the top of a short one?

If you could exhaust all the air from a very long tube, one end of which is in water, how high would water rise in it? The answer is about 34 feet on a clear day at sea level. This figure may be calculated in this way: The atmospheric pressure that will support your column of water is 14.7 pounds per square inch. The downward pressure of water is 0.433 pounds per square inch for *each foot* of the column of water. On dividing 14.7 by 0.433 we get approximately 34 feet. Try dividing these numbers yourself. Think about it.

Finally, you will try making water rise in a straw whose end is in water that is confined in an almost airtight coffee can. Does the closed container make any difference? Try it. Remember that the atmospheric pressure originally in the can is changed or weakened the moment water begins to rise up the straw. The air in the closed container is rarefied or thinned out as water leaves the can. Explain what happens then.

WHAT TO DO

... using atmospheric pressure to push a liquid up a tube

1. DO THIS

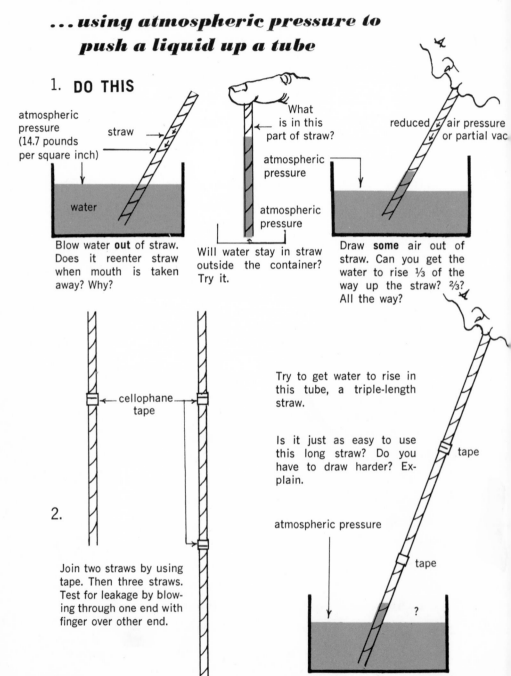

atmospheric pressure (14.7 pounds per square inch)

straw

water

Blow water **out** of straw. Does it reenter straw when mouth is taken away? Why?

What is in this part of straw?

atmospheric pressure

atmospheric pressure

Will water stay in straw outside the container? Try it.

reduced air pressure or partial vac

atmospheric pressure

Draw **some** air out of straw. Can you get the water to rise ⅓ of the way up the straw? ⅔? All the way?

cellophane tape

2.

Join two straws by using tape. Then three straws. Test for leakage by blowing through one end with finger over other end.

Try to get water to rise in this tube, a triple-length straw.

Is it just as easy to use this long straw? Do you have to draw harder? Explain.

tape

atmospheric pressure

tape

?

10

3.

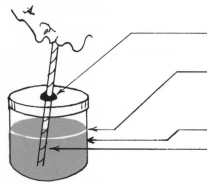

pinholes

Make pinholes in straw. Now try to get the water to rise in your straw. Explain what happens.

atmospheric pressure

Punch hole in plastic coffee-can cover with sharp nail. Then gradually enlarge hole with sharp end of a pencil until a straw fits in it **snugly.**

4.

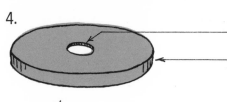

plastic coffee-can cover

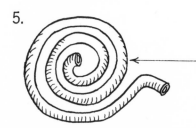

use chewing gum to prevent leakage

As water rises, does the pressure of the air in the can change? Explain.

coffee can

clean water

Now try drawing water up the straw. Is it more difficult than in an open container? Why? Try a double-length and then a triple-length straw. Explain your results.

5.

tube from a plastic jump rope

Straighten out the plastic tube and try to get water to rise in the tube all the way by using it as a straw.

11

WHAT YOU SHOULD KNOW

...about operating a group of siphons

You are going to connect the water in three different containers with siphons so that any change in the water level of one will immediately start a flow of water into or out of the other containers. The flow of water through the siphons will cease when the water level is the same in all the containers.

A siphon is a bent tube with unequal arms used for conveying a liquid over the edge of a vessel and delivering the liquid at a *lower* level.

You will start with a single siphon tube from which you will remove the air by filling it with water as explained on the experiment page. You will pinch the ends to close them, or press a finger against each end, and then quickly plunge the *shorter* arm into a glass of water. On releasing the other end, water will flow from higher to lower level. Why?

The top of the bend of your siphon tube cannot be higher than 34 feet. Try to give a reason for this statement. Do you think that the flow of water through a siphon would be more rapid if a large jar instead of a drinking glass were used — the depth of water in each vessel being the same? Try to find out by using a large jar.

The end of the *short* arm must always be underwater, else the action stops. Try raising this end slightly above the water level. Explain what happens.

12

Then try exposing the end of the long arm to the air while the siphon is working. Explain what happens.

In your arrangement of siphons connecting three containers with one another you will push each of the siphon ends down to the bottom of its container. If the levels are unequal, the flow will continue until the level is the same in each. Where are the long arms and short arms of the siphons now?

Remember that it is not the length of tubing underwater that matters but rather the distance from *water level* to top of the bend. Though the tubes in the above case have equal arms, the water flows because the *distance* from *water surface* to top of bend within one arm of the siphon is less than the distance from water surface to top of bend in the other arm of the siphon. In this case, with both siphon ends underwater, in which direction will the water flow? Why?

Finally, you will add a few measures or spoonfuls of water to one of the three containers in your siphon system. The action or resulting equalizing flow will be slow. Why? Give it a few minutes before checking on whether or not the levels in all three containers become the same.

You will also try removing some water from any one of the containers in your system. Compare the level in all three after a few minutes and explain what happened.

NOTE: Tubing, either rubber or plastic, may be obtained from various sources: the tubing used in a portable shower; the air-line tubing used in aquariums and sold at tropical fish stores; plastic jump ropes made of tubing; 1/4-inch rubber tubing sold in hardware stores.

WHAT TO DO

...arranging a group of siphons

1.

18-inch length of tubing
(see page 13 on where to obtain it)

fill tube with water to drive out air

Plug ends of tube with fingers. Turn tube over and make one arm **shorter** than the other. Place short end **under** liquid surface. Then release both ends as shown.

flow of water
atmospheric pressure

atmospheric pressure

Which way does the water flow? Why? When will the flow stop? Why?

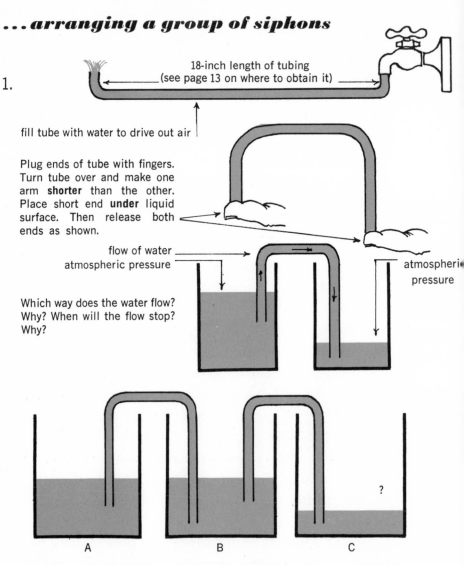

A   B   C

2.   Start with **A** full of water. Insert siphon tube leading water from **A** to **B**. When **B** is nearly half full, insert siphon tube leading water to **C**.

Observe levels in **A, B,** and **C** when system comes to rest or stops changing. Explain.

3.

measuring spoon

Use a **third** tube to connect the third glass with the first. Be sure **all** the ends of the siphon tubes are underwater and down to the bottom of the glasses.

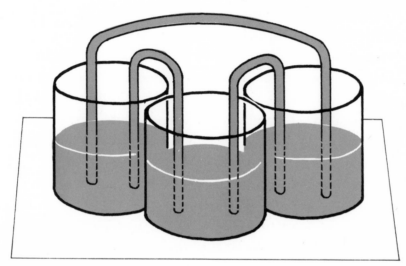

After the water level in all three glasses is the **same,** add the third siphon tube as shown above. Remember to fill it with water and insert ends in first and third glasses. Now add a few measures of water to **any** of the glasses. Do the levels soon equalize? Try adding the water to a different glass. Explain what happens.

4.

Use the above siphon system again. This time **remove** a few measures of water from any **one** glass. Wait to see if the levels equalize. Try removing some water from a different glass. Explain.

WHAT YOU SHOULD KNOW

...about balanced pressures

You are going to place an inverted drinking glass in a pan of water. You will notice that some water enters the glass. Since the air originally in the glass now occupies less space, is this air now under "extra" pressure? Explain.

To check your answer you will repeat the experiment, this time using an inverted paper drinking cup. While the cup is in the water you will cut a hole in its bottom. Now the air pressures inside the cup and outside the cup are the same — namely, atmospheric pressure, or about 15 pounds per square inch. Is the water level inside and outside the paper cup the same? Look into the cup and explain what you see.

You will try to equalize the air pressures inside and outside the same inverted glass by inserting a tube into the glass as described on the following pages. Will the water level inside rise to the level of the water outside the glass? Try it. Explain what happens. Will water always seek its own level when there are no interfering pressures? Why?

Next, you will *increase* the air pressure inside the same inverted glass by gently blowing air into it. Which pressure is greater now — the inside air pressure or the outside atmospheric pressure? What happens when you stop blowing air into the glass? Try it and explain what happens.

Remember that the atmospheric pressure on the surface of the water in the pan or bowl is transmitted by the water so that it acts upward on the inverted glass. If there is no air inside the glass — meaning that a vacuum exists there — then the atmospheric pressure outside will force the water up to the top of the glass or other container, provided the distance from outside water level to top of the inverted vessel is less than 34 feet. (See p. 9.) Explain this statement.

If there is a *partial* vacuum — that is, reduced air pressure — inside the inverted glass, then the outside atmospheric pressure will force water only part way up this glass. The liquid level inside the glass will come to rest when the combined air pressure *and* downward water pressure *inside* the inverted glass are equal to the atmospheric pressure outside. Think about this explanation.

You will try to raise the level of the water in the inverted glass by removing some air from within it, using mouth suction on an inserted tube. Does the water rise in the glass? Why? Will this water stay in the glass when the end of the tube is kept closed? When the tube's end is open to the outside air? Explain.

Finally, you will use a tube and mouth suction to remove practically all the air from the inverted glass. Will the glass fill with water? Why? Would the water rise to the top of *any* jar or bottle inverted and treated in the same way? Try using a container of a different size or shape and explain what happens.

WHAT TO DO

...balancing air pressures and water pressures in inverted containers

1. DO THIS

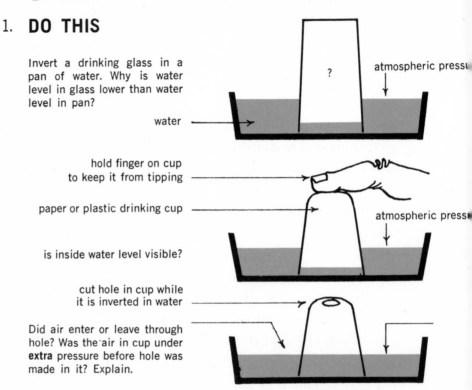

Invert a drinking glass in a pan of water. Why is water level in glass lower than water level in pan?

water

?

atmospheric pressu

hold finger on cup to keep it from tipping

paper or plastic drinking cup

atmospheric press

is inside water level visible?

cut hole in cup while it is inverted in water

Did air enter or leave through hole? Was the air in cup under **extra** pressure before hole was made in it? Explain.

2. Equalizing inside and outside air pressures.

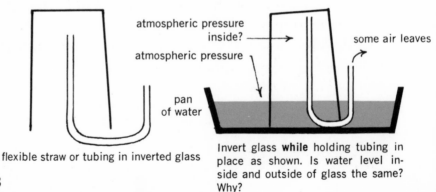

atmospheric pressure inside?

atmospheric pressure

some air leaves

pan of water

flexible straw or tubing in inverted glass

Invert glass **while** holding tubing in place as shown. Is water level inside and outside of glass the same? Why?

3. Effect of **increasing** the air pressure inside the inverted glass.

Blow gently into tubing. Why does the water leave the inverted glass? Take mouth away from end of tube. Explain what happens.

Repeat, but this time quickly place end of tube inside a bowl of water. Explain the air bubbles in bowl as water reenters inverted glass.

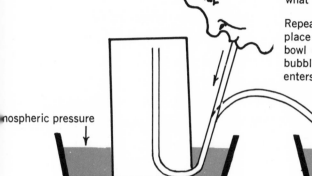

mospheric pressure

air bubble

4. Effect of **decreasing** the air pressure inside the inverted glass.

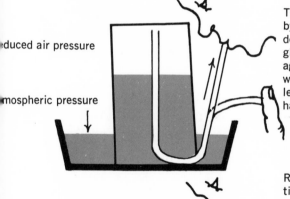

duced air pressure

mospheric pressure

This time draw air **out** gently by suction of your mouth. Why does water rise in inverted glass? Quickly press finger against end of tube. Explain why water stays in glass. Release finger pressure. What happens? Why?

Repeat the above, but this time bring water in inverted glass up close to top. Press finger against end of tubing and **quickly** remove tubing from glass without upsetting it. Will the water now stay in the inverted glass? Explain.

atmospheric pressure

19

WHAT YOU SHOULD KNOW

...about the flow of liquids out of inverted bottles

You are going to fill a wide-mouthed bottle (or a drinking glass) with water and then invert the bottle while holding a piece of cardboard against its mouth. Will the liquid stay in the bottle after you remove your hand? Try it. Does any water leak out of the inverted bottle? Can the cardboard be moved about horizontally without losing the water in the bottle? Try it.

You will then make one, two, and then three pinholes in the cardboard. Does the same experiment work equally well now? Explain. You will then try enlarging two of the holes in the piece of cardboard. Will the experiment work now? Will air bubbles enter and water leave the inverted bottle through the large holes? Explain what happens.

Remember that normal or atmospheric pressure is about 15 pounds per square inch at sea level. Atmospheric pressure can support about 34 feet — actually about 33 feet — of water in a vessel that is completely free of air or any other substance. (See page 9.) If some air is present, as in the case of your experiment with a half-full bottle of water, water will leak out until the air in the bottle thins out sufficiently to reduce the air pressure above the water in the inverted bottle. The atmospheric pressure on the cardboard will at all times, when there is no movement of the water, be equal to the downward pressure of the water in the bottle *plus* the reduced pressure of the air remaining in the bottle.

20

You will check on the above explanation by using a plastic drinking tube — or, if necessary, a transparent straw. In order to hold a liquid in a straw or narrow tube by the pressure of your finger on its upper end, some water must flow out of the straw. This loss of a few drops thins out the air inside the straw and reduces its pressure. You will mark off the water level in your straw to see if it changes.

Finally, you will fill a large soda bottle, one with a narrow neck, with water and then invert it over a sink. You will notice the gurgling sound caused by the intermittent flow out of the bottle. First, some water flows out. This reduces the air pressure over the water inside the bottle due to the thinning-out effect explained previously. The flow of water slows down or stops. A few air bubbles are then pushed into the bottle by the atmospheric pressure outside. These air bubbles increase the air pressure inside the bottle and the flow starts again. Soon this flow is interrupted as before and the entire process starts over again.

You can get the water to flow swiftly and smoothly from your narrow-necked bottle by inserting a piece of rubber or plastic tubing inside the bottle. The water, however, must be blown out of this tube as you invert it. Now there is a channel for the air to enter the bottle as water leaves it. Why does the gurgling stop now? Why does the water flow out so quickly when the tube is in place? Explain why liquids can be poured from wide-mouthed containers with no stoppage or gurgling, and from cans in which *two* holes have been punched.

NOTE: Plastic drinking tubes are inexpensive and can be purchased in drugstores. See note about obtaining tubing on p. 13.

WHAT TO DO

...using atmospheric pressure to speed the flow of liquids from containers

1. **DO THIS**

Hold cardboard firmly against bottle or drinking glass full, or half full, of water. Invert and take hand away. Does water stay in bottle or glass? Why?

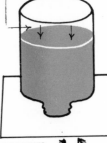

reduced air pressure

water

cardboard

atmospheric pressure

Make one, two, and then three pinholes in the cardboard. Will the water stay in the inverted bottles as before?

Enlarge two of the holes and try again. Any air bubbles in bottle? Any leakage? Explain.

2.

use a plastic drinking tube or light-colored drinking straw in glass of water

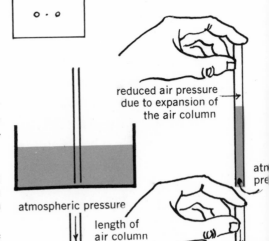

reduced air pressure due to expansion of the air column

atm
pre

length of
air column

atmospheric pressure

new water level

pre
wat

Place finger over bottom end of straw. Remove finger from top. Mark off water level on straw.

Replace finger over top of straw. Remove finger from bottom. Do any drops of water leave straw? Is air column within straw longer now? Has air pressure inside straw changed? Explain.

22

small drops o

3.

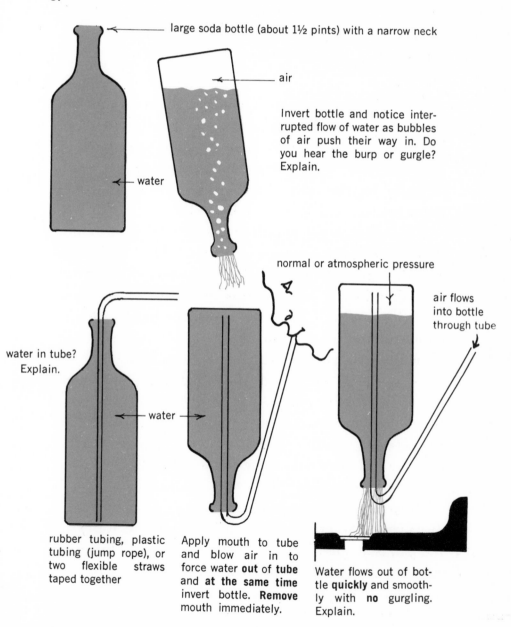

large soda bottle (about 1½ pints) with a narrow neck

air

Invert bottle and notice inter-rupted flow of water as bubbles of air push their way in. Do you hear the burp or gurgle? Explain.

water

normal or atmospheric pressure

air flows into bottle through tube

water in tube? Explain.

water

rubber tubing, plastic tubing (jump rope), or two flexible straws taped together

Apply mouth to tube and blow air in to force water **out** of tube and **at the same time** invert bottle. **Remove** mouth immediately.

Water flows out of bot-tle **quickly** and smooth-ly with **no** gurgling. Explain.

WHAT YOU SHOULD KNOW

...about a self-filling type of drinking fountain

You are going to make a drinking fountain that can be used by songbirds as well as by poultry. All you have to do is to invert a large jar in a pan of water. You will start with the jar about three-quarters full of water for the sake of simplifying the explanation, but a full jar will work equally well.

You will raise the mouth of the jar while it is underwater, so that the mouth rests on small blocks of wood. The thickness of these blocks determines the level of the water in the pan, for this level depends on how high the mouth of the jar is above the bottom. If the mouth of the jar rests on the pan bottom, there will normally be very little water in the pan. Why?

To speed up the process by which the pan is kept partly filled with water, you will do the following: Introduce a narrow tube or flexible drinking straw into the inverted mouth and gently blow a few air bubbles into the jar. Why does some water leave the jar as the air bubbles rise to the top?

Remember that here again there is a balancing of pressures. The atmospheric pressure on the water in the pan is about 15 pounds per square inch. This pressure, transmitted through the water in the pan, balances or supports two pressures present in the inverted jar: the downward pressure of the water in the inverted jar plus the (reduced) pressure of the air inside the jar. We might add that the column of water in the bottle that is supported by the outside pressure is measured from *surface* of water in the jar to *surface* of water in the pan.

You will try spooning some water out of the pan. What happens as soon as the surface of the water in the pan reaches the level of the mouth of the inverted jar? Try it. The moment you see one or two air bubbles rising in the jar it means that the air pressure inside the jar has increased. To balance this increase, some water has to leave the jar — it is forced out of the jar.

In this way the level of the liquid in the pan is kept more or less the same — that is, at the level of the mouth of the inverted jar. Gradually, over a period of a few hours or days, depending on the consumption of water, the inverted jar fills with air as it loses its water. It then must be refilled and reinverted in a pan of water. Try arranging a small fountain, using a half-pint jar, and set it aside on a shelf to see how long it takes for evaporation to empty the container.

A simple water barometer can be made from your drinking fountain by keeping the pan well filled with water to a set level and pasting a slip of paper on the jar as described in the next experiment. Daily changes in atmospheric pressure will cause corresponding changes in the level of the water inside the jar. Explain why this type of barometer is far from accurate.

If you stretched a strip of absorbent cloth from the pan of your fountain to the soil in a potted plant, would you have a self-watering system for your plant? Explain.

WHAT TO DO

...making a self-filling drinking fountain

1. reduced or less than normal air pressure

   large wide-mouthed jar or jug

   atmospheric pressure

   pan of water →

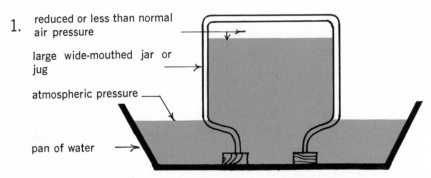

   wood blocks to raise mouth of bottle above bottom of pan

   Fill jar with water and then invert it in a pan of water, using a piece of cardboard to keep water from escaping while inverting. Slip cardboard out. Slide two wood blocks under mouth of jar without allowing any air to enter jar.

2. Study the effects of entering air bubbles.

   blow a few air bubbles **into** jar

   As air bubbles rise, is the air pressure inside bottle increased or decreased?

   atmospheric pressure

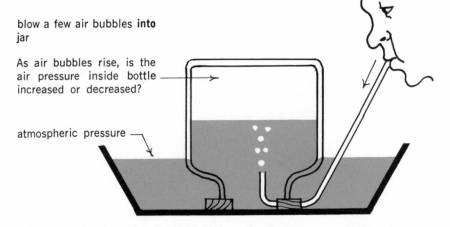

   Can you get water to move down the jar into the pan by blowing air into the bottle? Explain.

3. What happens when water in the pan is consumed, or evaporates on standing?

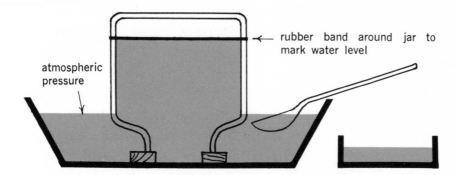

atmospheric pressure

rubber band around jar to mark water level

Carefully begin to spoon out some water from the pan. Keep on spooning out water until the tops of the wood blocks are exposed. Now, do air bubbles enter the jar as you continue? Why? Does any water leave the jar? Can you spoon **all** of the water out of the pan? Explain.

4. Can your drinking fountain be used as a barometer?

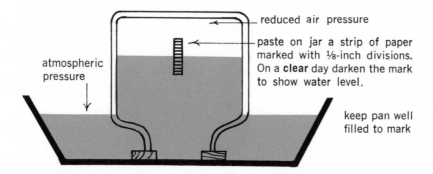

reduced air pressure

paste on jar a strip of paper marked with ⅛-inch divisions. On a **clear** day darken the mark to show water level.

atmospheric pressure

keep pan well filled to mark

Will water level in jar fall on a stormy or cloudy day? Why? Will level rise again as weather clears? Is this type of barometer accurate? Explain.

WHAT YOU SHOULD KNOW
...*about using steam to*
produce a partial vacuum

You are going to invert a pint canning jar in a pan of water. On boiling the water in the pan, steam will rise in the jar and gradually force most of its air out. Will some of the air in the inverted jar leave it because of expansion due to heat? Explain.

When the pan is removed from the burner, water will begin to rise in the inverted jar as it cools. Does the water move halfway up the jar? Three-quarters of the way up? Try it and explain why it rises at all.

Remember that when steam at 212°F changes back to water at 212°F there is a great reduction in volume. The *water* formed by the condensation of this steam occupies 1/1700th of the volume the steam had occupied. There is therefore a sharp reduction in the atmospheric pressure within the inverted jar. As a result, the atmospheric pressure on the surface of the water in the pan pushes water up the jar.

Think of the straw experiment (page 8). Instead of reducing air pressure by the suction of your mouth, you reduce the air pressure in the inverted jar first by filling it with steam and then cooling the steam so as to turn it back to water. Any space in which there is less than normal pressure is said to contain a *partial vacuum*.

Our purpose here is to show how atmospheric pressure can be utilized to keep the lid pressed so firmly against the mouth of a canning jar as to make the jar airtight. Once the jar and its contents have been sterilized, it is important that no air leak into the jar, for this would introduce micro-organisms and thus cause spoilage.

To learn how this airtight seal can be achieved, you will half-fill a canning jar with water and place it *right side up* in a pan of water. After boiling the water in the pan as directed, you will remove the jar from the pan (USE A TOWEL TO AVOID BURNING YOUR FINGERS) and *quickly* apply a self-sealing canning lid to the mouth of the hot jar. Also screw down the metal band over the lid. On cooling, will the steam in the jar condense as before? Will air enter? Explain.

After the jar is cool you will remove the screw band and try to pick up the jar by grasping the lid only. If you have a good partial vacuum under the lid, then the latter will support the weight of the jar and its contents.

Once the jar is cool, atmospheric pressure acting on the outer surface of the lid will push the lid tightly against the rim of the jar. Remember that atmospheric pressure is about 15 pounds per square inch on all surfaces. Suppose your lid is 4 square inches in area. Then 60 pounds of force are pressing down on the lid — that is, if no air at all is present under the lid. Suppose only half the air in the jar has been forced out? What will then be the force acting to keep the lid pressed down? Explain.

NOTE: Do *not* consider the above as directions on how to can foods. Our purpose here is only to investigate the part played by atmospheric pressure in keeping such jars airtight. Specific canning directions are available in bulletins from the U.S. Department of Agriculture and from the Extension Services in the different states.

NOTE: Self-sealing lids and screw-top rings can be purchased at most hardware stores.

WHAT TO DO

...producing a partial vacuum within a jar

1. Forcing some of the air out of the jar.

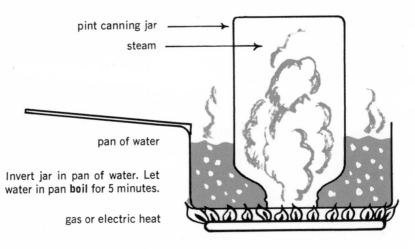

pint canning jar

steam

pan of water

Invert jar in pan of water. Let water in pan **boil** for 5 minutes.

gas or electric heat

2. After jar cools.

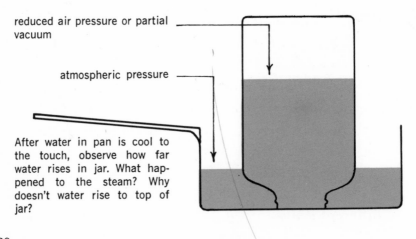

reduced air pressure or partial vacuum

atmospheric pressure

After water in pan is cool to the touch, observe how far water rises in jar. What happened to the steam? Why doesn't water rise to top of jar?

3. Using steam to expel some air from jar.

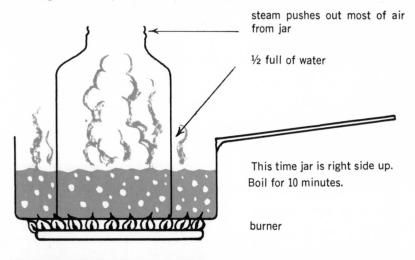

steam pushes out most of air from jar

½ full of water

This time jar is right side up. Boil for 10 minutes.

burner

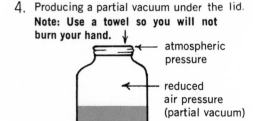

sealing compound

brass screw band

YOU WILL NEED: Flat canning lid with a sealing-compound border and a brass screw band.

brass lid fits mouth of jar

4. Producing a partial vacuum under the lid. **Note: Use a towel so you will not burn your hand.**

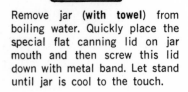

atmospheric pressure

reduced air pressure (partial vacuum)

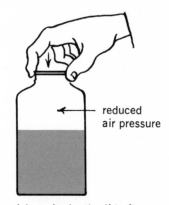

reduced air pressure

Remove jar **(with towel)** from boiling water. Quickly place the special flat canning lid on jar mouth and then screw this lid down with metal band. Let stand until jar is cool to the touch.

Try to pick up jar by the lid after removing the screw band. Does the lid hold? What really keeps the lid on tightly?

WHAT YOU SHOULD KNOW

...about measuring the change in volume when water freezes

You are going to test your experimental skills by finding the percentage increase in volume when water solidifies. Instead of using a cube of water you will work with a narrow column of water inside a drinking straw.

The plastic straw, of course, will have room at the top for the water to expand when it freezes. The water you will add to the straw must be as close to 4°C (39°F) as possible. Why? Remember that water steadily contracts as it cools to this temperature. If you use water above this temperature, it will contract after you put the straw in the freezer and will soon be lower than the level you marked on the straw. Think about this.

The information you are seeking is no secret: any good science textbook will inform you that when a cubic inch or a cubic foot or a cubic centimeter of water at 4°C is frozen, it will expand by about 9% of its original volume. Another way of saying exactly the same thing is that water increases by 1/11th of its original volume when it changes to ice.

In your experiment you will carefully note only the change in length of the column of water, a cylinder within the straw, when it solidifies. Since you are working with a cylinder any change in length will keep in step with the accompanying change in volume — that is, will be proportional to the change in volume. Of

32

course, we are assuming that the straw itself does not contract or expand while in the freezer. Read this paragraph again and think about it.

Try to think of other ways in which errors may creep into this experiment. Remember that the probability of errors is always considered in measurement or quantitative experiments. One must either allow for these errors in the calculations or reduce their impact on the results as much as possible. Consider this one: The ice in the straws, while still in the freezer, is at a temperature below the freezing point of water — that is 0°C. Will this ice begin to expand the moment the straw is taken out of the freezer? Explain how you would minimize this possible error.

Let us say that in dividing the two lengths to get your results, as explained in the next experiment you arrive at the quotient 1.13. What does this number mean? It means that the *1 unit* in your straw, regardless of its particular length, expanded to 1.13 units. In other words, the increase in volume was 0.13, or 13 per cent. Do not expect to arrive at the 1.09 figure with no trouble at all. Since you are working without a thermometer and with the simplest materials, an expansion figure between 1.04 and 1.14 should be regarded as evidence of good work. Keep at it. Don't stop with one or two trials.

We might add that the force exerted by the expansion of freezing water is enormous. Steel bombs filled with water have been burst by exposing them to below-freezing temperatures on cold winter nights.

NOTE: Your metric scale or ruler is marked off in centimeters and millimeters. If a length is 11 cm. and 4 mm., then write it as 11.4 cm., etc.

WHAT TO DO

...finding the fractional increase in volume when water freezes

1. short plastic straws

    3 short straws, each about 16 cm. long, cut from plastic drinking straws. A **small** chewing-gum plug is sufficient.

    about 16 cm.

    chewing-gum plug

Add 3-4 ice cubes to the water you will use in the experiment.

2. **NOTE:** You must work **fast** in this part. Place each straw in freezer **as soon** as it is filled and marked.

    about 4 cm.

    use pipe cleaner to remove air bubbles from water in straw. **Mark** off water level on straw with pencil or ink line.

    about 12 cm.

    Add ice-cold water to each straw up to about 4 cm. from the top.

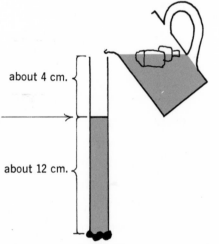

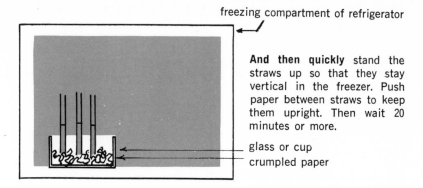

freezing compartment of refrigerator

And then quickly stand the straws up so that they stay vertical in the freezer. Push paper between straws to keep them upright. Then wait 20 minutes or more.

glass or cup
crumpled paper

3. Mark off ice level **immediately.** Do measuring afterward.

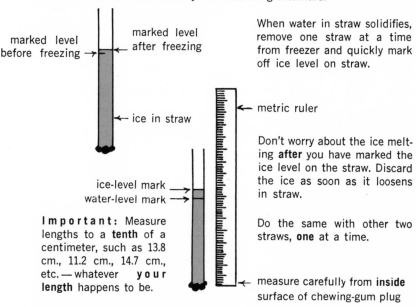

marked level before freezing →

marked level after freezing ←

ice in straw ←

metric ruler ←

When water in straw solidifies, remove one straw at a time from freezer and quickly mark off ice level on straw.

ice-level mark →
water-level mark →

Don't worry about the ice melting **after** you have marked the ice level on the straw. Discard the ice as soon as it loosens in straw.

I m p o r t a n t : Measure lengths to a **tenth** of a centimeter, such as 13.8 cm., 11.2 cm., 14.7 cm., etc. — whatever **y o u r length** happens to be.

Do the same with other two straws, **one** at a time.

measure carefully from **inside** surface of chewing-gum plug ←

4. How to calculate the fractional increase in volume when water changes to ice:

$$\frac{\text{length of ice column in centimeters}}{\text{length of water column in centimeters}} = ?$$

Divide the two lengths as indicated above. Do this calculation separately for each straw. Are your results close to 1.09? Try averaging your three results. Note that 1.09 means 1 unit of volume + 0.09 of a unit of volume.

WHAT YOU SHOULD KNOW

...about the transparency of ice

You are going to investigate the clarity of ice. As you know, ice is sometimes transparent or almost as clear as glass, while at other times it is white or translucent. You will freeze disklike shapes of ice from faucet water, boiled water, and, finally, from unflavored soda water.

Remember that a substance is transparent when you can see objects through it clearly, distinctly. A translucent substance is one that lets some light pass through it but not enough for objects to be seen distinctly. Glass is an example of a transparent substance; a frosted light bulb is an example of a translucent substance.

You are aware that water drawn from a faucet usually contains dissolved air. The air bubbles appear when a glass of water is allowed to stand for a while in a warm room. Are these air bubbles responsible for the whiteness or translucency of ice cubes, or of the disk of ice in your experiment with faucet water?

To find the answer to the last question, you will boil the faucet water to drive out the dissolved air and then place the *pan* containing the water in your freezer. Pouring it into another container may introduce air into the boiled water. Will ice formed from boiled water be transparent? Try it.

The temperature of your freezing compartment is usually well below 0°C (32°F), the freezing temperature of water. As a result, the water in your samples freezes rapidly. This rapid freezing causes the air under the surface ice layer to be trapped before it can escape. The whiteness or translucency of the ice, when all of it solidifies, is due to this trapped air rather than to dissolved air in water. Does the freezing of water, whether in a saucer or in an ice-cube tray, start with a thin layer of ice at the *top* or at the *bottom*? Find out by inspecting the water in an ice-cube tray at frequent intervals after putting the tray in your freezer.

You will remove the thin layer of ice that is the first to form and hold it close to newsprint. Can you see the letters clearly? Is this ice transparent? Explain.

Finally, you will pour some unflavored soda water into a saucer and freeze the soda water as before. Is ice formed from soda water whiter than ice formed from ordinary water? Try it, and then explain what you see.

Soda water contains dissolved carbon dioxide, a tasteless, colorless gas. When bottled under pressure and capped, soda water may contain as much as four volumes of this gas in solution. This means that a bottle of soda water contains about four bottles of dissolved carbon dioxide.

When the cap is removed from a soda-water bottle, most of the gas bubbles out and escapes into the air. But one volume, or a bottleful of the carbon dioxide, still remains in the water. Do you think the presence of this gas in the soda water, plus the usual air under the frozen surface layer, account for the white color of the ice formed from soda water? Explain.

WHAT TO DO

...investigating the clarity of ice

1.

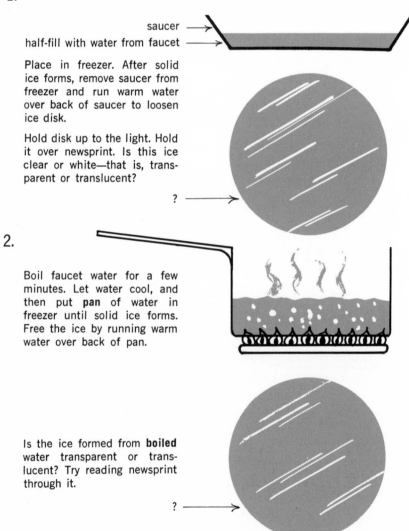

saucer →

half-fill with water from faucet →

Place in freezer. After solid ice forms, remove saucer from freezer and run warm water over back of saucer to loosen ice disk.

Hold disk up to the light. Hold it over newsprint. Is this ice clear or white—that is, transparent or translucent?

? →

2.

Boil faucet water for a few minutes. Let water cool, and then put **pan** of water in freezer until solid ice forms. Free the ice by running warm water over back of pan.

Is the ice formed from **boiled** water transparent or translucent? Try reading newsprint through it.

? →

3.

Start again with faucet water as before.

Place in freezer, but this time take it out **as soon as** a **surface** layer of ice forms.

Remove the **thin** disk of ice and hold it close to newsprint. Is this ice transparent or translucent? Explain.

There may be a hole in the thin layer. This does not matter.

clear or white?
thin surface layer of ice

Try the same experiment with boiled water and also with distilled water (or rain water).

carbon dioxide bubbles
clear soda water

4.

Do gases in water, such as carbon dioxide, make ice appear white?

Pour some clear soda water into a saucer. Freeze the soda water solid, as before.

Hold this disk of soda-water ice close to newsprint. Is the ice formed from soda water transparent or translucent? Explain.

?

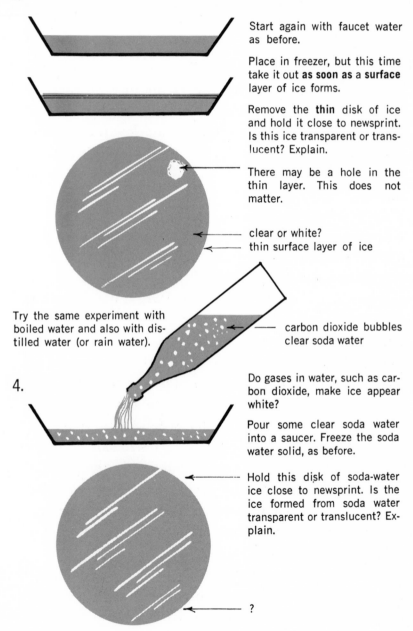

WHAT YOU SHOULD KNOW

...about fractional freezing

You are going to dissolve table salt in water and then try to remove some of the water from this salt solution by a method called *fractional freezing*. This means that you will expose the salt solution to a low temperature until a layer of ice forms at the surface. Will the layer of ice taste salty? Try it. Taste the salt water under the ice.

In general, the freezing point of water is *lowered* when anything is dissolved in it. In other words, it takes a lower temperature to freeze salt water than it does to freeze fresh water. The mixture you made by dissolving salt in water is called a *solution*. Pure water freezes at 0°C (32°F). Your salt solution freezes a few degrees below this temperature.

Before deciding whether or not the ice formed on the surface of your salt water is pure, or free from salt, you will press it to remove some of the liquid. Now taste the ice again. Is the salty taste still present? Explain. Remember that when ice forms in salt solutions some of the salt water is entangled within the pores of the ice. For example, the ice formed from sea water contains about one-fifth of the salt originally present in sea water. Explain what happens when you press or squeeze the ice in your experiment.

In your freezer, usually close to 20°F, the temperature of your salt-solution sample slowly falls below the freezing point of the solution. Ice begins to form. As this ice separates, the liquid surrounding it becomes saltier or more concentrated. Why? The freezing point of this more concentrated salt solution therefore drops. Does this explain the saltier taste of the solution left after the surface ice is removed? Remember that it is only the water that freezes in your experiment. The freezing point of a saturated *salt solution* is $-22°C$ ($-7.6°F$), a temperature your freezer cannot reach.

You will dissolve a teaspoon of sugar in a cup of water and treat it in the same way. Will the surface layer of ice formed by the partial, or fractional, freezing taste sweet? Try it before and after squeezing the sugar solution out of the ice. Explain the change, if any, in the sweetness of the sugar solution remaining after ice forms.

Finally, you will try two other solutions — bicarbonate of soda (baking soda) dissolved in water, and black coffee right from the pot before sugar or cream have been added. In the former case, the bitter taste of the bicarbonate will tell you whether the ice formed from its solution is pure or mixed with the solution. In the coffee solution there will be present dissolved caffeine (1 to 2 per cent), caffeol — an oily substance that gives the desired aroma, and also glucose, dextrin, and protein. Your ice may have a slightly yellowish tint. Why? Be sure to taste the ice before and after squeezing out the coffee solution. Also compare the taste of the coffee solution left in the cup after removing the ice with the original taste of the coffee. Explain your results.

WHAT TO DO

...removing water from a solution by fractional freezing

1.

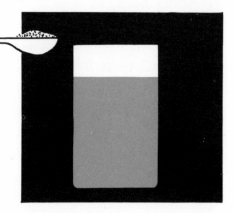

Add ½ tsp. of table salt to a glass of water. Stir until all of the salt dissolves. Taste the salt water.

Pour some of your salt solution into a small measuring cup. Place cup in freezer or freezing compartment of your refrigerator. Wait about 15 minutes.

small aluminum measuring cup ⟶

2. Remove cup from freezer **as soon as** a layer of ice forms on the surface of the salt solution. **Do not** allow the contents of the cup to freeze solid.

solidified layer of ice ⟶

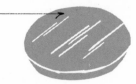

Use a knife to remove the ice layer. Taste it. Is it salty? Try squeezing it gently. Taste it again. Any difference? Explain. Also taste solution left in the cup. Is there any change in taste? Explain.

3.

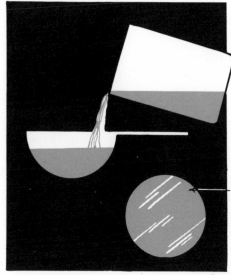

Add 1 tsp. of sugar to a glass of water. Stir until all the sugar dissolves.

Pour some of your sugar solution into small cup as before. Place in freezer until a **layer of ice** forms on surface.

solidified layer of ice

Remove ice layer. Taste it. Is it sweet? Try squeezing sugar solution out of it. Taste it again. Explain. Taste liquid in the cup. Compare its sweetness now with original taste. Explain.

4.

bicarbonate of soda

pot of percolated coffee

aluminum cup

solution of bicarbonate of soda

Dissolve ½ tsp. bicarbonate of soda in water.
Place in freezer until **layer** of ice forms on surface.

Taste this ice. Press liquid out and taste again. Taste solution left in cup. Explain.

"black" coffee from pot

Place in freezer until layer of ice forms on surface.

Is this ice yellowish? Press it between tissue paper. Any change? Explain.

Taste this ice. Press coffee solution out of it. Taste ice again. Explain. Taste the coffee remaining in cup. Is it stronger or weaker than original coffee? Explain.

43

WHAT YOU SHOULD KNOW

...about separating substances from solutions by distillation

You are going to dissolve a solid — table salt — in water and then try to recover some of the pure water from the salt solution. You will boil the salt water and then hold a cold plate over the vapor given off by the boiling solution. Will the drops forming on the cold plate be salty or tasteless? Try it and then explain your results.

When you boil your salt water, the water in the solution changes to a vapor. On being cooled by the cold plate, this vapor changes back to a liquid. This process, consisting of evaporation followed by condensation of the vapors in a separate container, is called *distillation*. As we shall see, it is possible to recover the solvent — that is, the pure water in your salt solution — and also to separate mixed liquids by means of the distillation process.

Remember that when a solid such as table salt is dissolved in water and then heated, the vapor that rises contains *none* of the dissolved substance. You will also try sugar solution, another example of a solid dissolved in a liquid. When the vapor rising from the hot sugar solution is cooled by the dinner plate, condensation occurs. You will taste these drops and then explain what you find.

The method you are using is distillation in its simplest and crudest form. In laboratory distillations, the vapor rising from the heated liquid passes through a long tube that is surrounded by cold running water. This tube is called a *condenser*. The special flask or retort in which the liquid mixtures is boiled is usually provided with a thermometer.

You next will work with a solution of a liquid in another liquid. What happens when a mixture of liquids is heated? To find out, you will boil cider vinegar, which consists of about 96 per cent water and 4 per cent acetic acid. We shall disregard the minute amount of coloring and flavoring material. Water boils at 100°C, while acetic acid boils at 118°C. Which vapor will come off first — water vapor or acetic acid vapor?

Since the boiling points are fairly close to one another, *both* vapors will appear at the same time, but there will be a greater proportion of the liquid with the *lower* boiling point. Will the drops of liquid that condense on the plate taste slightly sour or very sour? Try it. Will the vinegar left in the pot after some of it has been distilled taste stronger or weaker? Try it. Note that in this case it is the water that has the lower boiling point.

Actually, the effective separation of liquids in a mixture when they boil at neighboring temperatures is not possible except by *fractional distillation*. This is accomplished in specially designed stills where separate fractions of the distillate — condensed vapors — are collected at different temperatures.

Finally, you will try your hand at the simple distillation of percolated coffee. In this case the solution contains solids such as caffeine, glucose, dextrin, and protein as well as an aromatic oil called caffeol (very low boiling point). Can pure water be separated from this coffee solution by simple distillation? Try it.

WHAT TO DO

...separating substances from solutions by distillation

1.

Dissolve ½ tsp. of salt in a cup of water.

Pour your salt solution into a **large** pan and boil vigorously.

Turn flame off and **quickly** place cold, clean, dry dinner plate on pan for a few seconds.

Remove plate, and taste drops formed on its undersurface. Are they tasteless? Salty? Explain.

2.

Dissolve 1 tsp. of sugar in a cup of warm water.

Pour sugar solution into a large pan and boil vigorously.

Turn flame off and quickly place cold, clean, dry dinner plate on pan for a few seconds.

Taste the drops formed on undersurface of plate. Are they tasteless? Sweet? Explain.

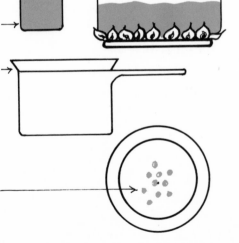

3.

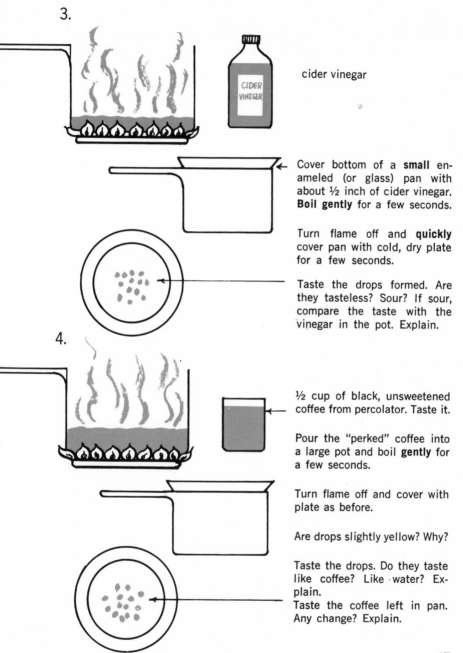

cider vinegar

Cover bottom of a **small** enameled (or glass) pan with about ½ inch of cider vinegar. **Boil gently** for a few seconds.

Turn flame off and **quickly** cover pan with cold, dry plate for a few seconds.

Taste the drops formed. Are they tasteless? Sour? If sour, compare the taste with the vinegar in the pot. Explain.

4.

½ cup of black, unsweetened coffee from percolator. Taste it.

Pour the "perked" coffee into a large pot and boil **gently** for a few seconds.

Turn flame off and cover with plate as before.

Are drops slightly yellow? Why?

Taste the drops. Do they taste like coffee? Like water? Explain.
Taste the coffee left in pan. Any change? Explain.

WHAT YOU SHOULD KNOW

...about the melting and refreezing of pieces of ice in warm water

You will begin by suspending two ice cubes from threads and then bringing the cubes into light contact. Will the ice cubes freeze together after a few minutes? Try it and then explain what happens. Also try contact between an edge and a flat surface, between edge and edge, etc.

The above experiment was first made by Faraday (1791–1867), English physicist, in an effort to understand the phenomenon of regelation, or refreezing. The process of melting under pressure and freezing again as soon as the pressure is relieved is known as *regelation*. The best known experiment on regelation, in which a wire with heavy weights attached gradually works its way down through a block of ice, was also devised by Faraday.

You will lower a suspended ice cube until it just touches a small piece of ice floating in water. Will the extremely light pressure cause the small piece of ice to freeze to the lower surface of the upper piece? Try it.

Next, you will float two ice cubes in *warm water*. When near each other, the floating cubes will be attracted and move close together. Has capillarity anything to do with this attraction? (See page 56). Now observe carefully what happens between the cubes — that is, where the edge of one touches the side or edge of the other. Use a flashlight if necessary.

See if your floating cubes behave as follows: The parts in contact freeze where they touch. The surrounding *warm* water causes rapid melting of the ice at the place of contact. However, the two pieces of ice, at the end of the melting process, continue to be united by a *narrow bridge of ice*. Soon this connecting bridge melts, after which the pieces separate for a few moments and immediately draw together again. Then the entire process begins again: freezing, melting at place of contact, formation of the bridge, and so on. This "rhythmic" series of steps is repeated until the ice disappears.

The English scientist Tyndall (1820–1893), like Faraday, doubted whether the accepted explanation of regelation could be applied to these warm-water experiments. The pressures involved in these experiments are minute, and not at all like those in the weighted wire passing through a block of ice. He pointed out that an increase in pressure on the ice cubes of one atmosphere, or 14.7 pounds per square inch, will lower the melting temperature of ice by only $0.007°C$. Also, that the cold water formed from the ice by pressure does not freeze, but moves right into the warm water.

Finally, you will break a few ice cubes into several irregular pieces and then float them in warm water. It is interesting to watch the delicate bridges form, melt away, and then form again after the pieces make contact once more.

Another explanation offered is that capillary forces between blocks of ice draw the blocks together with enormous resulting pressure. But in your warm-water experiments any sharp point will form a bridge whether in contact with a flat surface or with another sharp point. How would you explain refreezing in warm water?

WHAT TO DO

...investigating the melting and refreezing of ice in warm water

1.

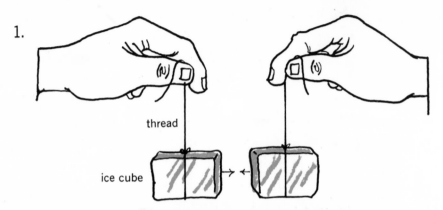

thread

ice cube

While suspending the two ice cubes in air, bring them into contact. Keep the pressure as light as possible. Do the cubes freeze together after a few minutes? Explain.

2.

Lower the suspended ice cube until it just meets the small piece of floating ice. Do the two pieces freeze together after a few minutes of contact? Explain.

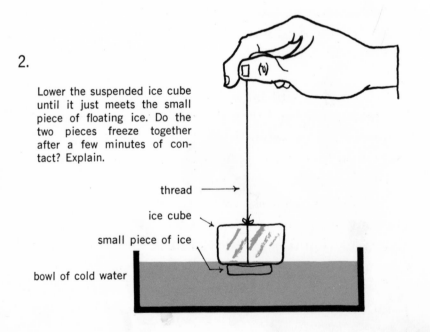

thread →

ice cube

small piece of ice

bowl of cold water

3.

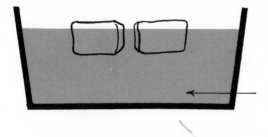

Place two ice cubes in warm water. Are the two cubes attracted to each other? Why?

bowl of warm water

"bridge" of ice

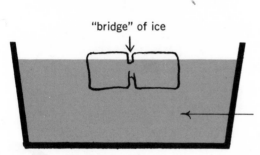

Wait a few minutes. Do the cubes freeze together where they touch? Does ice at place of contact begin to melt, leaving a "bridge"? What happens after the cubes break away? Observe and explain.

warm water

4. **looking down into bowl**

Place two ice cubes in a towel and then break the cubes into several pieces.

Observe what occurs. Be patient and watch carefully.

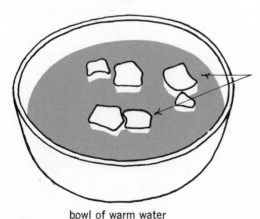

pieces of ice

Do you see the following? · · ·

Attraction and freezing?

Melting and bridge-forming?

Complete separation and then new contact?

Refreezing and then melting again?

bowl of warm water

51

WHAT YOU SHOULD KNOW

...about the shape assumed by a free liquid

You are going to place a drop of olive oil on a glass plate. The drop will lose its spherical shape as it flattens out against the glass because of the force of gravity. Try to explain this last statement.

You will try dropping olive oil into cold water. Here it will float on the water surface because the oil is lighter (less dense) than water. Does the pull of gravity make the drops lose their spherical shapes? Look through the side of the container and explain what you see.

You will drop olive oil into a small glass of "rubbing" alcohol. In this case the olive oil is heavier (denser) than the alcohol. Will the drops settle to the bottom of the glass? Try it. Examine the drops of olive oil after they come to rest. Are they flattened at the bottom? Why? You will try stirring the mixture so that the olive-oil drops float about for a few moments. Are there any changes in the shapes of the oil drops now? Explain.

Remember that the surface of the olive oil, or of any other liquid, has a tendency to contract because of cohesive forces between like molecules. This contractile force is the cause of the spherical shape of a liquid drop. Why a sphere? Because this is the shape in which the drop has the least surface. Another way of saying it is this: The geometric figure that has the smallest surface area for a given volume is a sphere.

You are going to drop olive oil into a bottle in which a layer of alcohol rests on a heavier (denser) layer of water. The oil drops, whose density is less than that of water but greater than that of alcohol, will settle and remain suspended near the boundary level. Will the oil drops assume an almost perfect spherical form? Try it and explain what you see. Note that olive oil is *not* soluble in water or in cold alcohol.

Remember that a floating body, as in the alcohol-water experiment, *apparently* loses its entire weight. The drop of oil is thus a free liquid and hence assumes its natural shape — a sphere. Fogdrops, raindrops, and minute *floating* particles of all liquids are very nearly spherical. Why?

Drops of liquid do not have to float in order to form spheres. For example, mercury spilled on a table will form small globules that are almost perfect spheres, and falling drops of molten metal will assume spherical shapes. Why? Keep in mind that as a body of liquid becomes smaller and smaller the gravitational forces acting upon it become less and less.

The dewdrops on spider webs and on the downy leaves of plants are tiny spheres. Can you explain why? The contractive force that causes these drops to be spherical is called *surface tension.*

Caution: Be sure to keep the "rubbing" alcohol away from children. Discard the alcohol if children are around, because they might mistake it for water. This type of alcohol is *poisonous if taken internally.*

WHAT TO DO

...suspending drops of oil within a liquid

1.

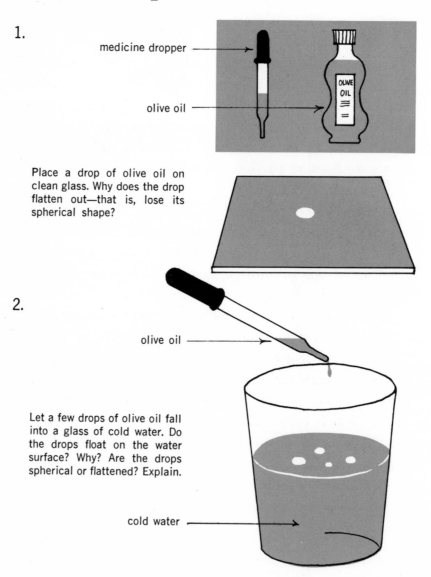

medicine dropper

olive oil

Place a drop of olive oil on clean glass. Why does the drop flatten out—that is, lose its spherical shape?

2.

olive oil

Let a few drops of olive oil fall into a glass of cold water. Do the drops float on the water surface? Why? Are the drops spherical or flattened? Explain.

cold water

3.

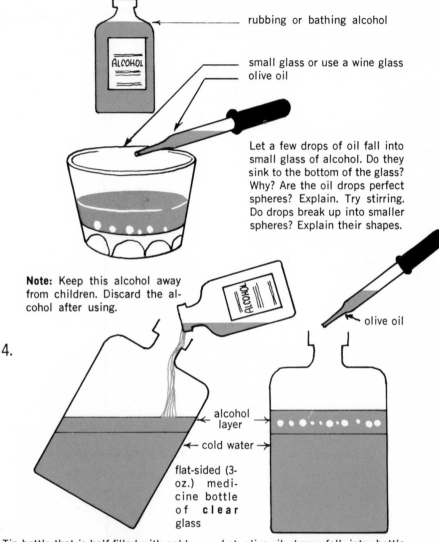

rubbing or bathing alcohol

small glass or use a wine glass
olive oil

Let a few drops of oil fall into small glass of alcohol. Do they sink to the bottom of the glass? Why? Are the oil drops perfect spheres? Explain. Try stirring. Do drops break up into smaller spheres? Explain their shapes.

Note: Keep this alcohol away from children. Discard the alcohol after using.

4.

olive oil

alcohol layer

cold water

flat-sided (3-oz.) medicine bottle of **clear** glass

Tip bottle that is half-filled with cold water and carefully add about ⅓ as much rubbing alcohol. Let alcohol run down side so as not to disturb the water beneath it. **Do not** shake or stir.

Let olive-oil drops fall into bottle. Why do oil drops float within the alcohol layer? Do the drops seem to be perfect spheres? Explain. Set bottle aside and examine again a day or two later.

WHAT YOU SHOULD KNOW

...about the attraction between floating bodies

You are going to float two clean strips of wood in water. Will the two pieces of wood, which are wet by water, attract each other when they come close together? Try it.

You have often observed that sticks, logs, and other drifting materials tend after a time to cling to one another. In your experiment you will try to tow one piece of wood by pulling on the other, with only the attractive force holding the two together.

You also will investigate the attractive forces between floating corks, floating pieces of a drinking straw, and any other light objects you may have at hand. Try the towing test in each case.

If you look carefully between the floating objects that are *wet* by water, you will observe that the water level between two such floating objects when close together is higher than the level of the water in the basin. The rise of liquids in small tubes and in interstices, or narrow spaces, is due to surface tension (see page 53). A general name for this phenomenon is *capillarity*.

This elevation of the water level between the two pieces of wood in your experiment accounts for the attractive force between them. The water level between the floating objects is higher than the outside water level — that is, the level of the water in the basin. Remember that pressure in a liquid decreases with height. The pressure at the outside level and on the outside of the floating objects is atmospheric or about 15 pounds per square inch. The pressure at the inside level must therefore be less than 15 pounds per square inch. Since the outside pressure is greater, the pieces of wood are pushed together.

You will try the experiment with objects that are *not* wet by water, such as two paraffin wax blocks. Will the wax blocks be attracted and cling to one another? Try it.

Keep in mind that liquids are *depressed* in narrow tubes or spaces when they do *not* wet them. Examine the space between the blocks of wax when they seem to be in contact. Is the water level in this very narrow space elevated or depressed relative to the water level in the basin?

A depressed water level between the wax blocks will cause the pressure there to be less than on the outside of the blocks. Will the blocks be pushed together — that is, attracted? Try it and explain your results.

Finally, you will float an object that is wet by water alongside one that is *not* wet by water. You will use a strip of wood and a block of wax. Try moving the objects alongside one another so that they almost touch. Wait and see what happens. Will they remain in contact or will they separate because of repulsion? Try it.

To sum up: Two floating objects that are wet by the liquid supporting them will attract one another. Two floating objects that are *not* wet by the liquid will also attract one another. In the case of two floating objects, one of which is wet by the liquid and the other not wet by the liquid, there will be repulsion.

NOTE: Paraffin wax, which is used for canning, is inexpensive and available at most hardware stores.

WHAT TO DO

...towing floating objects by the attractive forces between them

1. Objects wet by water

Two strips of wood separated from a spring clothespin. Wash in soapy water and rinse. Or use any two clean strips of wood.

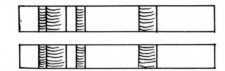

Tie a thread to a tack or small nail hammered into one wood strip.

water

basin or large bowl

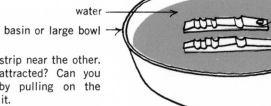

Bring one strip near the other. Are they attracted? Can you tow one by pulling on the other? Try it.

2. Objects wet by water

2 corks washed in soap and water

straight pin in one cork with thread attached

two pieces of drinking straw

tie thread through pinhole in straw

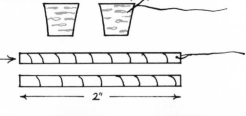

2"

Do corks drift together and cling? Try towing one cork by pulling the other. Explain.

Do straw pieces attract each other when close? Can the free straw be towed by the other? Try it. Explain.

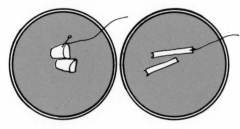

3. Objects **not** wet by water

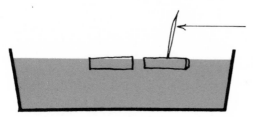

square the sides with a clean knife

two small (about 1½-inch) blocks of paraffin wax

Wash loose particles away from blocks of paraffin under running cold water.

insert toothpick in one block

Bring the wax blocks alongside each other. Any attraction? Can you tow one by making contact with the other?

4. One object wet by water, the other **not.**

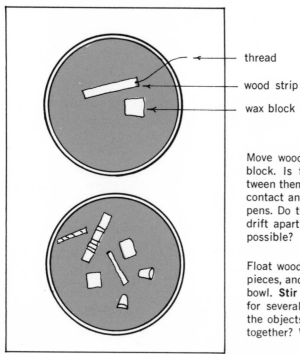

thread

wood strip

wax block

Move wood strip close to wax block. Is there attraction between them or repulsion? Make contact and observe what happens. Do they stay together or drift apart? Explain. Is towing possible?

Float wood strips, corks, straw pieces, and wax blocks in **large** bowl. **Stir** and then let stand for several minutes. Which of the objects will gradually drift together? Why?

WHAT YOU SHOULD KNOW

...about the motions of bits of camphor on a clean water surface

You are going to scatter small bits of camphor (*not the naphthalene crystals used in making moth balls*) on the surface of the water in a clean glass. The floating camphor particles will immediately begin to spin and move about irregularly. These movements will continue for an hour or longer if your water and container are absolutely clean.

Remember that a liquid tends to reduce its exposed surface to a minimum (see page 52). Because of this tendency, the surface of a liquid acts as if it had a thin elastic membrane stretched over it. The name given to this contractive force on liquid surfaces is *surface tension*.

As your camphor bits dart about over the water surface, they gradually dissolve in the water, thereby reducing the surface tension of the water. The camphor bits are irregular in shape; the sharp points or edges dissolve faster than the rounded parts. Thus the surface tensions around each particle of camphor are not equal on all sides. These unequal forces cause the camphor bits to spin and dart about. Each particle of camphor moves in the direction of the strongest tension — that is, *toward* the side on which the *least* camphor is dissolved.

You will then start again with another glass of water and fresh camphor bits. This time you will scatter chalk dust on the surface of the water. The movements or paths of the camphor particles will be easier to follow as they plow their way through the chalk dust.

NOTE: Small squares of synthetic camphor are inexpensive and may be purchased at any drugstore. *Keep the camphor away from children.* They might think the white camphor is candy and try to eat it.

A lack of movement on the part of your camphor particles indicates that either the water or the container is contaminated with oil or grease. If this occurs, discard the contents of the glass and start again with a glass that has been washed in detergent solution.

The effect of even the slightest amount of oil on your camphor experiment is easily demonstrated. The oil left on a pin that has come into contact with your hair is sufficient to stop the motions of the camphor bits.

So sensitive are the camphor particles to the presence of oil on the water surface that the term "camphor point" is used to denote the minimum thickness of the oil layer that will stop the movements of camphor particles. Lord Rayleigh (1842–1919), English scientist, found that an olive oil film about two-millionths of a millimeter thick is capable of stopping the movements of camphor particles. He suspected that this figure is close to the diameter of the oil molecule. In a later experiment he determined that the diameter of the oil molecule is about half the thickness noted above. Today we know that the oil molecule is not spherical and that Rayleigh was measuring its long dimension.

Can the movements of the camphor bits be started again after having stopped because of the presence of oil? You will carefully move a piece of clean tissue paper across the water surface so as to absorb some of the oil. Will the bits begin to spin again? Try it.

WHAT TO DO

...investigating the motions of bits of camphor on water

1. small block of synthetic camphor

Dig out a small piece of camphor (about ⅛ inch) with a **clean** knife. Wash hands before touching the camphor. (See note on obtaining camphor on page 61)

Place the piece of camphor between two strips of paper and crush it by pressing down. **Do not** touch the camphor with the fingers.

2. Wash glass **thoroughly** with detergent to free it of oil or grease. Rinse. Add cold, clean water. Drop bits of crushed camphor on surface of water.

looking down into water

Notice the spinning, irregular motions of the bits of camphor. These go on for an hour or more. If not, oil or grease must be present. Discard, wash glass, and try again.

Scrape chalk with a razor blade or knife and let chalk dust fall on water surface while camphor bits are moving about. Are the paths taken by the spinning bits of camphor more visible now?

chalk

3.

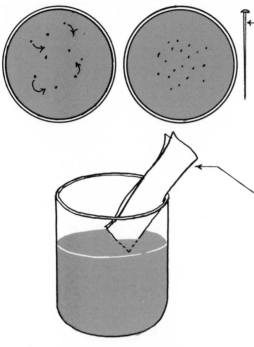

 pin

(a) Start over again with a clean glass, clean water, and fresh camphor.

(b) Pass a pin through your hair two or three times. Plunge pin momentarily into the water and remove. Do the camphor bits immediately stop moving? Explain.

facial tissue

(c) Carefully run tissue paper across the surface of the water two or three times to remove some of the oil. Do the camphor bits begin to spin and move about again? Explain.

4.

clean pieces of camphor

½-inch piece of wooden matchstick

cut slit in one end of matchstick and insert piece of camphor in it

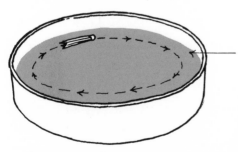

Large bowl filled with water. Be sure to wash the bowl in detergent and rinse.

Is the tiny "boat" propelled around on the water surface? Why? If motion is slow, **clean** the water surface with facial tissue, as in part 3(c) above.

cold water

WHAT YOU SHOULD KNOW

...about the flow of water from a hose

You are going to find out how much water flows out of a hose per second or per minute with a given setting of the hose nozzle and outside faucet. This figure is called the rate of discharge from the hose. To do this you will check the time and then fill a pail with water. The number of seconds it takes to fill a 10-quart pail, for example, will enable you to calculate the rate of discharge from your hose.

You will determine the rate of discharge with the nozzle set to deliver a fast jet — that is, a fast, narrow stream of water. You will then remove the nozzle *while* the water is running through the hose so as not to change the setting at the faucet connection. Once again you will fill the same pail and keep track of the number of seconds required. In which case will the rate of discharge be higher — when there is a nozzle present to produce a fast jet or when there is no nozzle to throttle the discharge? Try it and then explain your results.

Keep the following in mind: A nozzle is a converging tube. A jet is a stream issuing from an orifice. The stream of water from your nozzle is called a *free* jet because it is surrounded by air and is under the influence of gravity. The purpose of the nozzle is to convert fluid pressure into velocity. However, in throttling the stream of water passing through the nozzle, some of the pressure energy is used to overcome friction within the nozzle. Does this last fact help to explain why it takes somewhat longer to fill the same pail with water in one part of the experiment than in the other?

Another way of putting the last question is this: Will a pail fill more quickly when the hose delivers a wide, slow-moving stream of water than when the hose delivers a narrow, fast-moving stream?

The next experiment with the flow of water from a hose is to find out how far, measured horizontally, you can reach with a stream of water. This horizontal distance, measured on the ground, from the nozzle to where the stream strikes the ground is called the *range* of the jet.

As explained in the illustrations on the next page you will use a sheet of cardboard on which 0°–90° angles have been marked off. Keeping the same nozzle setting, you will change the angle of the nozzle slowly and note how far the stream reaches on the ground. Does the range increase as the angle increases? Or does the range increase gradually and then decrease? Try it — on a summer day, of course.

The trajectory or path of your liquid jet is under the influence of gravity. This means that it will follow a downwardly curving path. The curve is approximately a parabola.

Ideally, the maximum range of your jet or stream is achieved at an inclination of 45°. However, this angle is reduced because of air friction and the spreading of the jet. About a 30° inclination of the nozzle will yield the maximum range. Your maximum range, or greatest horizontal distance, may be a few degrees more or less than 30°. Try it. Have a friend place markers, such as small stones, at places where the stream from the hose strikes the ground during the trials.

NOTE: To convert from gallons per minute to cubic feet per minute use this fact: 1 cubic foot = 7.48 gallons.

WHAT TO DO

...measuring rate of discharge and range of a stream of water

1. Rate of discharge from nozzle.

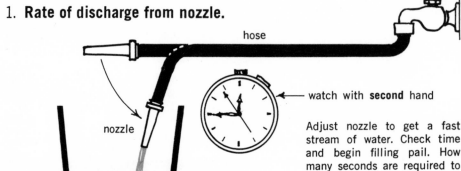

hose

nozzle

watch with **second** hand

pail (10-qt. size) or use any container of known capacity

Adjust nozzle to get a fast stream of water. Check time and begin filling pail. How many seconds are required to fill pail to the very top? Do it two or three times and average your results. How many quarts of water per **second** flow out of nozzle? Or multiply **quarts per second** by 60 and get **quarts per minute.**

2. Rate of discharge from nozzle.

end of hose with nozzle removed

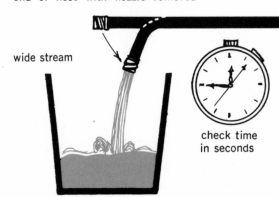

wide stream

check time in seconds

Without changing setting of outside faucet or valve, remove the nozzle **while** water is running through it. Fill same pail again. How many seconds are required without the nozzle? Do it two or three times and average your results.

Compare the number of quarts per second now with the previous trial. Explain. Or multiply **quarts per second** by 60 and get **quarts per minute.**

3. Marking off angles on a board.

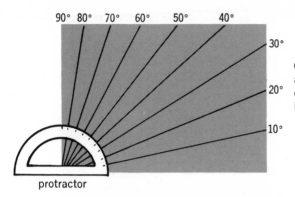

90° 80° 70° 60° 50° 40°
30°
20°
10°

protractor

On a cardboard (or plywood) about 1½ feet × 2 feet, mark off angles as shown with the help of a protractor.

4. Finding range at different angles to ground.

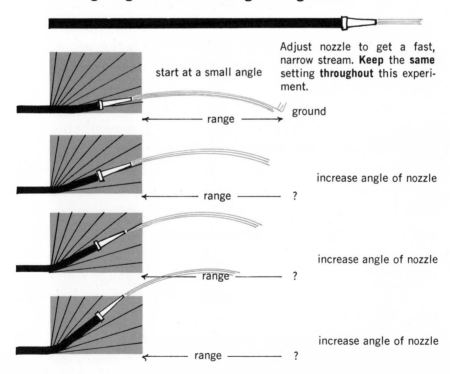

start at a small angle

Adjust nozzle to get a fast, narrow stream. **Keep** the **same** setting **throughout** this experiment.

range ——→ ground

range ——— ?

increase angle of nozzle

range ——— ?

increase angle of nozzle

range ——— ?

increase angle of nozzle

Mark the angle of the nozzle at which the stream of water reached its maximum horizontal distance or range. Then measure the angle exactly with a protractor. How many degrees? Make several trials.

WHAT YOU SHOULD KNOW

...about the Cartesian diver

You are going to make a Cartesian diver, which was invented by Descartes (1596–1650), the French philosopher. The diver itself is usually made of a small hollow glass image in human shape. You will make yours out of a medicine dropper. When floated in a bottle of water that is tightly covered by a stretched rubber membrane, the diver can be made to sink or rise at will by pressing on the membrane.

You will start by drawing a little water into the dropper. This added weight will stabilize it so that it will float vertically. You will know that you have added the correct amount of water to the dropper when it floats vertically and deeply — that is, with the top of the rubber bulb *just showing* above the surface of the water in the bottle.

After securing the rubber membrane to the top of the bottle, you will try pressing down on the membrane with your finger. The dropper should start down slowly. If it does not move, add to the amount of water *inside* the dropper so as to bring it slightly lower when in floating position. Now reattach the rubber membrane and try again.

When your diver is operating properly, notice the level of the water inside it. Does this level change when the diver moves down from the top or up from the bottom of the bottle of water? Explain.

Remember that air, a gas, is a compressible fluid. The pressure of your finger on the rubber membrane will compress the air under the membrane as well as the air locked inside the dropper. When your finger pressure is reduced, or entirely relieved, the air within the dropper returns to its original volume.

Liquids, on the other hand, are practically incompressible. The pressure added to the surface of the water in the bottle when your finger compresses the air under the membrane is transmitted through every part of the water and acts on all surfaces in contact with the water. In this case the liquid is not free to flow except up the stem of your medicine dropper.

When water rises slightly up the stem of the medicine dropper its *total* weight — glass, water, air, rubber bulb — increases. It can no longer float, because it now weighs more than a volume of water of the same size and shape as the medicine dropper. When the finger pressure ceases, the air inside the dropper expands and water leaves the dropper. The dropper rises. Why?

Archimedes (287?–212 B.C.), the famous Greek mathematician, developed an explanation of the above. According to his principle, if the total weight of the body (dropper) is greater than that of an equal volume of water, the dropper sinks. If the weight of the dropper is less than that of an equal volume of water, the dropper will be forced upward.

Any object partly or completely immersed in a fluid is buoyed up by a force equal to the weight of the fluid displaced. A ship afloat displaces its own weight of water. Fish can change the upward pressure or buoyant forces acting on them by changing the *volume* of water they displace. For this they utilize "swimming bladders," which can be expanded or compressed at will. How is the total weight of a modern submarine changed?

NOTE: Medicine droppers may be purchased at drugstores. Ask for the four-inch size.

WHAT TO DO

...making a Cartesian diver

1.

clear-glass soda bottle (about 1-qt. size)

medicine dropper (4-inch size)

Piece of ½-inch adhesive tape about 2 inches long. Mark it off with lines about ⅛ inch apart. Apply it lengthwise along medicine dropper.

Cut out 3″ × 3″ section from toy rubber balloon.

2.

Draw some water into dropper.

Put dropper in bottle. If it sinks, there is too much water in it. Invert bottle, remove dropper, squeeze some water out of it, and try again.

Keep adjusting the amount of water in dropper until it floats with its top almost level with the surface of the water in bottle. Once you accomplish this, place finger over top of bottle and tip bottle to let some water out.

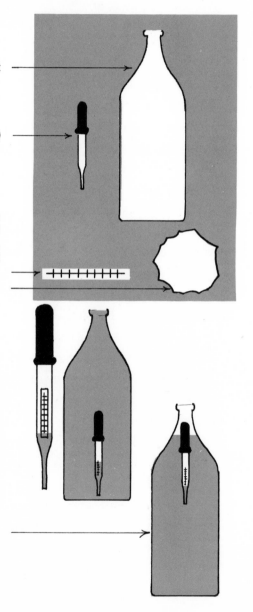

3.

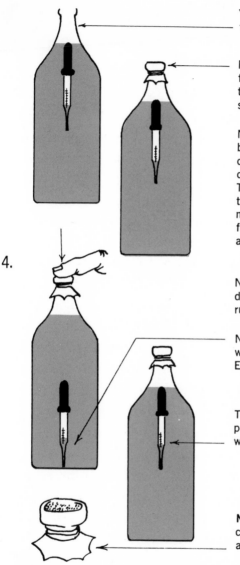

Your bottle should look like this.

Fasten piece of rubber sheet from balloon across top of bottle. Use rubber band to keep sheet taut and flat.

Now press down hard on rubber cover with finger. The dropper should gradually move downward. Take finger away. The dropper should move to the top again. If there is no movement, your dropper is floating "too high." Remove it, and draw more water into it.

4.

Note the water level **inside** dropper, then press down on rubber top.

Note water level inside dropper when latter sinks to bottom. Explain.

Take finger off top. Does dropper rise? Why? Is there less water in dropper now? Explain.

Note: If rubber sheet becomes concave, loosen rubber band and pull taut again.

5. Repeat the above, but this time observe the level of the water in the **dropper** when dropper **opening or end** moves down 1 inch, 2 inches, 4 inches, etc. Explain.

WHAT YOU SHOULD KNOW

...about finding the specific gravity of certain floating solids

You are going to use a quick, simple method for finding out how many times a particular floating solid is as heavy as water. In all your experiments the answer or result will be less than one, since your solids will float in water. Explain. This method gives a quick estimate, but can only be used when the floating solid is in the shape of a rectangular block and does not dissolve in water.

Specific gravity, an ancient term, is the ratio of the weight of a substance to the weight of an equal volume of water. The temperature of the water used as the standard for one comparison is usually either 4°C (39°F) or 20°C (68°F); the latter temperature is room temperature. In recent years the term *relative density* has been substituted for specific gravity since gravity has nothing to do with these ratios.

In your experiments you will float rectangular blocks of different materials — wood, cork, paraffin wax, etc. — in water. All you have to do is to determine what fraction of the floating object is immersed or underwater. If half the block is underwater, then the material is half as heavy as an equal volume of water — hence its specific gravity is ½ or 0.5. If it floats with seven-tenths of its volume underwater, then its specific gravity is $\frac{7}{10}$ or 0.7, and so forth.

This method, applicable only to floating objects, is faster than other methods, but not as accurate. The reason for the inaccuracy is that it is difficult to measure the exact level to which the floating body sinks in water. Try it and you will understand why. However, the depth-of-immersion method does give a good approximation, particularly if you first mark off the edge of the blocks as explained on the next pages.

Remember that when your block of wood or other material is floating in water it has pushed aside or displaced a volume of water equal to the weight of the block. According to Archimedes' principle (see page 69), a floating body displaces its own weight of the liquid in which it floats.

Suppose your block of wood, for example, floats half-immersed in the water. This means it has pushed aside a rectangular block of water with exactly the same dimensions as the bottom of your wood block but *half* as thick or high. Why not the same thickness? The water displaced, since it is half as thick or high as the wood block, must therefore weigh as much as the entire wood block. Explain. Thus the wood block must weigh as much as a "block" of water *half* its size. Therefore the wood block must weigh half as much as a block of water equal to it in shape and volume. The specific gravity of this particular kind of wood must be ½ or 0.05. Reread this paragraph two or three times and think about it.

Here is a specific gravity list for some common floating solids:

oak: 0.7–0.9	balsa wood: 0.2	(water = 1.00)
pine (white):	cork: 0.24	ice: 0.92
0.38–0.4	paraffin: 0.8–0.9	
pine (yellow):		
0.54–0.72		

WHAT TO DO

...estimating the specific gravity of certain floating solids

1. Use a rectangular block of wood (pine, for example) about 3″ × 2″ × ¾″. Mark off the thickness, or ¾-inch dimension, with 12 marks at 1/16-inch intervals made with either a ballpoint pen or a pin.

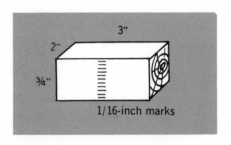

1/16-inch marks

How deeply does your block of wood sink in the water? **Or** how "high" does it float? **Example:** If there are 12 marks along its thickness and it floats with 6 marks **underwater,** then the block of wood weighs 6/12, or ½, as much as an equal volume of water. Therefore, the specific gravity of the wood you used is **0.5.**

Work **quickly.** The wood may absorb water.

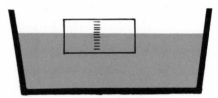

basin of water

2.

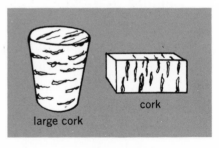

large cork   cork

Cut and sandpaper the cork to the shape of a rectangular block. Mark off thickness by dots at 1/16-inch intervals. Make dots with a toothpick or pin.

Specific gravity of cork equals the number of **dots underwater divided** by the number of dots in full thickness.

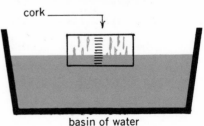

cork

basin of water

3. Try a rectangular block of oak or walnut or balsa (or any wood you have at hand). Be sure to cut the block squarely. The thickness may be more or less than ¾ inch. Be sure to mark the thickness with **equally** spaced dots or lines.

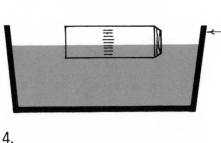

Suppose there are 10 marks along the thickness and 7 of them are underwater. Then the specific gravity of this variety of wood is 7/10 = 0.7.

Or: Sp. Gr. = $\dfrac{\text{number of dots underwater}}{\text{number of dots in full thickness}}$

4.

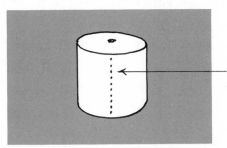

pinholes 1/16-inch apart

Short piece of a **thick** candle (a cylinder). It must float upright.

block of paraffin wax

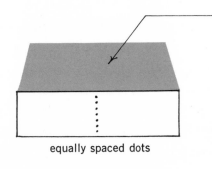

equally spaced dots

Float each of the above in water. Find the specific gravity in each case. Or substitute any other lighter-than-water **and** insoluble-in-water materials you may have on hand.

WHAT YOU SHOULD KNOW

...about pressure due to the weight of a liquid

Your experiments here will be concerned with a stream of water issuing from a hole in the side of a plastic bottle or plastic jug. The range of this stream is the horizontal distance traveled by the stream. You will compare the range of a stream issuing from a large container with that coming from a smaller one — when the distance from *hole* to *water surface* in both containers is the same. Will the range be greater in the case of the larger container? Try it.

The pressure you are investigating is called gravity pressure, because it is caused by the weight of the fluid itself. In any given liquid this pressure increases with depth. At any one place in a liquid the pressure is equal in all directions. At any one level within a liquid the pressure is the same at all points. In your experiment the water pressing against the wall of the container at right angles pushes the water squarely through the hole or opening.

The range of a stream in your experiment does *not* depend on how much water there is in the container — that is, the volume of water. It does *not* depend on how much water there is below the level of the hole. The range depends only on how far the hole is from the surface of the water; in other words, it depends on *depth*. As the stream of water keeps coming out of the hole in the side of the container, the level of the water in the container falls. Will the range, or horizontal distance reached by the stream, change? In what way? Explain.

Next, you will investigate the dozen or so streams issuing from a circle of holes parallel to the bottom of the container. Do these streams appear to have more or less the same range? Explain. Suppose you arrange a circle of holes higher up in the same container. Which will have a greater range — the upper or the lower circle of streams? Why?

Finally, you will pierce several holes, about one inch apart, along a vertical line on the side of a plastic container. Study the different streams issuing from these holes. Is there a difference in range? Explain your results.

Remember that the actual pressure in *different* liquids is *not* the same at the same depth. The pressure within a liquid depends not only on depth but also on the density of the liquid. For example, the pressure one inch below the surface of mercury, a heavy liquid, is equal to the pressure about 13 inches below the surface of water. Try to explain this statement. Note that the density of mercury is 13.6 grams per cubic centimeter, while the density of water is 1 gram per cubic centimeter. Density is the mass per unit volume of a substance.

If you allow water in a container to issue vertically from a small hole or orifice, you will observe an interesting phenomenon. The vertical jet of water rises to nearly the level of the free surface of the liquid in the container from which it flows. The Italian scientist Torricelli (1608–1647) discovered and explained this phenomenon in the course of his investigations of fluid motion.

WHAT TO DO

...investigating the range of an emerging stream of water

1. plastic gallon or half-gallon jug after cutting off upper part to remove handle

   plastic bottle (pint or quart size)

   Mark each container as shown with lines 5 inches apart. Use thick pin or needle to make a smooth round hole in each on lower line. Plug the holes with chewing gum.

   5"

   hole   hole

2. **Fill** plastic bottle with water. Place bottle next to kitchen sink. Mark position of edge of bottle. Remove plug. Quickly place bowl so that stream strikes it in center the moment the water level in bottle reaches **upper** line.

   upper level line →

   mark corner position on drainboard

   sink

   ← small bowl

   Leave the bowl in position. Fill the jug and remove plug as above. Then observe where the stream strikes at the moment the water level reaches the **upper** level. Which stream has the greater range? Does the stream reach the center of the catch bowl? Explain.

   marked position same as above bowl

78

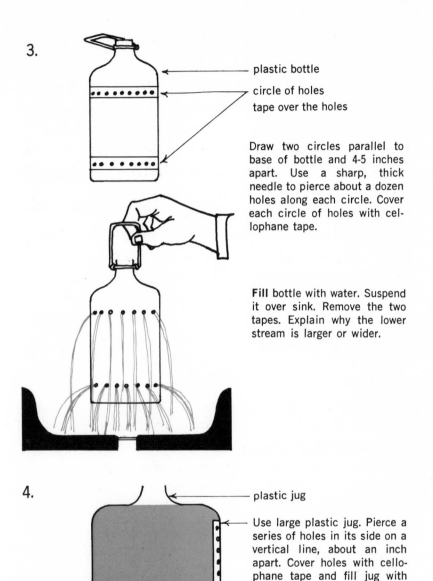

3.

plastic bottle

circle of holes
tape over the holes

Draw two circles parallel to base of bottle and 4-5 inches apart. Use a sharp, thick needle to pierce about a dozen holes along each circle. Cover each circle of holes with cellophane tape.

Fill bottle with water. Suspend it over sink. Remove the two tapes. Explain why the lower stream is larger or wider.

4.

plastic jug

Use large plastic jug. Pierce a series of holes in its side on a vertical line, about an inch apart. Cover holes with cellophane tape and fill jug with water. Will the **ranges** of the different streams be equal or unequal? Explain. Remove tape and test theory.

sink drainboard

WHAT YOU SHOULD KNOW

...about making water wetter

You are going to place four separated drops of water on waxed paper. The upper surface of each drop will be curved, even though the curve of the lower surface is flattened by gravity. The drops do not spread out and wet the paper nearby because the surface layer in each acts like a stretched elastic membrane. (See experiments on surface tension, page 53).

You will now add a few soap particles to the surface of one drop of water, a few particles of detergent powder to the second drop, and a tiny drop of detergent solution to the third. Will the substances you add serve to lower the surface tension of each drop of water? If this happens, the drop will flatten out as water spreads out and wets the paper around the drop. Try it.

To find out what happens when water is in contact with grease or fat, you will form two separate rings of butter on waxed paper and add a drop or two of water to the interior of each ring. Will the water wet the surrounding butter? Try it. You will make the water wetter in *one* case by sprinkling a few particles of soap on the surface of the drop of water. Will the soap gradually increase the wetness of the water so that the water will spread over or through the surrounding butter? Try it. Observe whether this drop flattens out and loses its rounded shape. Explain what happens.

Detergent is the general term for substances used in cleaning — lye, soap, washing soda, etc. In recent years chemists have created new substances that are more effective in some ways than traditional detergents.

80

These new cleansing agents are called *synthetic detergents*.

You will place two drops of oil on waxed paper. On one drop you will deposit a smaller drop of water; on the other you will deposit a smaller drop of water containing dissolved detergent. Does the pure water spread over the oil surface? Does the detergent-solution drop spread over the water surface? Explain what happens.

In this last case the reaction is on the boundary layer between the oil and water surface. This boundary layer is called an *interface*. Keep in mind that the lowered surface tension — and therefore increased wetting ability of water containing dissolved detergent — exists not only on the external surface of the water but also wherever it meets oil or any liquid with which it does not readily mix.

The cleansing action of soaps and other detergents on "soils" — meaning grease-enclosed dirt particles — involves a complex process. The important fact is that your detergents are effective surface-active agents — that is, they lower the surface tension of the washing solution; they also reduce the interfacial tensions between non-mixing, or immiscible, liquids such as oil and water. This increases the wetting ability of the solvent — for example, the water used in your experiments — and thus assists in the penetration of the materials to be cleaned. The addition of a small amount of soap to water at 25° C reduces the surface tension of water to about one-third of its original level.

Finally, you will try applying detergent particles directly to the surface of oil drops. Detergents lower the surface tension and increase the wetting property of liquids in which the detergents *dissolve*.

WHAT TO DO

...making water wetter

1. Place 4 drops of water, each about ¼ inch in diameter, on waxed paper. Use a medicine dropper or piece of drinking straw to do this. Do the drops appear spherical or rounded at the top? Why?

   Dissolve some detergent in water to obtain a detergent solution. Then use flat end of a toothpick or matchstick and add a few particles of soap, a few detergent particles, and a small drop of detergent solution to three of the drops of water. Keep the drops under observation for several minutes. Is there any evidence of change in surface tension or "wetness" of the water? Explain.

   small drop of detergent solution

   use small magnifying glass to observe what happens in drops

drops of cold water on waxed paper

soap particles (use granulated soap or shave particles from cake of soap)

untreated water drop

particles of powdered detergent

2. water drop within ring of butter

   Use a toothpick to arrange two **rings** of butter, about ¼ inch in diameter, on waxed paper. Place a few drops of water inside each ring. Does the water wet the butter? Add more water to drops until they are higher than the rings of butter. Now add the soap particles to **one** drop. Observe what happens after a few minutes. Does the soap cause any change in the surface tension or in the "wetting" ability of the water? Explain.

   waxed paper

   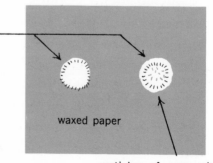
   particles of soap placed on surface of water drop.

3.

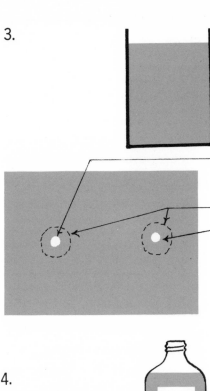

dissolve ½ tsp. of cold-water detergent in glass of water

small drop of water

large oil drop (about ⅜ inch in diameter)

small drop of water containing dissolved detergent

Use olive oil or corn oil, and place two large drops on waxed paper. Add small drop of water to one drop of oil and small drop of detergent solution to the other. Does pure water wet the surface of the oil drop? Does water containing detergent wet the surface of the oil drop? Observe for several minutes, using magnifying glass if possible. Explain what happens.

4.

two large drops of oil

particles of detergent

drop of liquid detergent

waxed paper

This time use **only** oil drops. Sprinkle either soap or detergent particles over the surface of **one** of the drops. Add a small drop of concentrated liquid detergent to the other. Do the oil drops begin to spread or "wet" the paper? Explain.

83

WHAT YOU SHOULD KNOW

...about cleansing power or detergency

You are going to investigate the cleansing action of soaps and synthetic detergents on oily "dirt" such as is commonly present on clothing worn next to the skin.

You will allow a few drops of oil to make their way up through water and a detergent solution, respectively. Even before stirring you will notice that the oil drops are fewer but larger in diameter on the water surface than on the surface of the detergent solution. When you try to push the drops together, the oil drops on water will unite or merge to form still larger drops; the oil drops on detergent solution will resist merging and, instead, break up into still smaller drops on being pushed together. Why?

Next, you will try shaking each sample vigorously in a bottle. Remember that oil and water are immiscible liquids, meaning they do not mix. However, the shaking itself breaks up the oil into tiny droplets dispersed throughout the surrounding liquid in each case. Such a dispersion of one liquid in another is called an *emulsion*. In the case of the oil droplets dispersed in water, the emulsion lasts for a short time; on standing, the oil and water soon separate into two distinct layers.

In your other sample, the detergent dissolved in the water tends to stabilize the emulsion and make it permanent. This means that the droplets of oil suspended in the solution are prevented from uniting or merging even when they rise to the surface. Soaps and synthetic detergents dissolved in water act as *stabilizers* in oil-water emulsions.

Keep in mind that the molecules of soaps and synthetic detergents are chainlike in structure. One end of each molecule has an affinity, or attraction, for the water and the other end for oil. Thus one end of this type of molecule dissolves in the droplet of oil and the other end remains in contact with the water surrounding the oil drop. As a result, each oil droplet is coated with soap or detergent molecules, the water-soluble ends of which are pointing outward. It is for this reason that the oil drops in a stabilized emulsion do not unite; in fact, the water-soluble ends of the molecules extending into the water have *like* electric charges and therefore repel one another. This repulsion keeps the oil droplets suspended in the water.

To understand how the above applies to the cleansing process, you will "launder" two strips of soiled gauze, in each of which solid dirt particles have been covered with oil. In the bottle containing warm water and either dissolved soap or detergent there will be a lowering of the surface tension of the water as well as of the interfacial tension between oil and water within the solution (see page 81). This assists in the penetration and wetting of the fabric.

The detergent or soap molecules help to emulsify the oil on the fabric and float it away. Then the clumps of solid dirt particles are broken up by the wetting action of the solution. Finally, both oil drops and solid particles are suspended in the soapy water or in the detergent solution during agitation and washed away during the rinsing cycles. Explain the appearance of the dirty gauze washed in pure hot water and compare it with the piece washed in soapy water or in detergent solution.

WHAT TO DO

...emulsifying and suspending "oily dirt" by the action of detergents

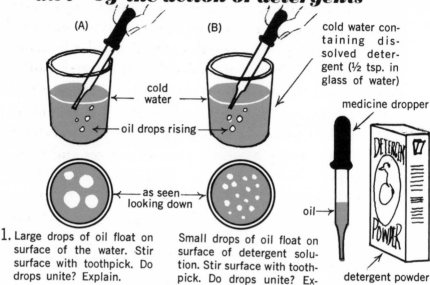

(A)

(B)

cold water

← oil drops rising →

as seen looking down

cold water containing dissolved detergent (½ tsp. in glass of water)

medicine dropper

oil →

detergent powder

1. Large drops of oil float on surface of the water. Stir surface with toothpick. Do drops unite? Explain.

Small drops of oil float on surface of detergent solution. Stir surface with toothpick. Do drops unite? Explain.

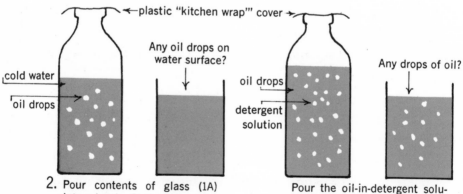

← plastic "kitchen wrap'" cover →

cold water

oil drops

Any oil drops on water surface?

oil drops

detergent solution

Any drops of oil?

2. Pour contents of glass (1A) into a bottle. Shake vigorously. Then pour mixture back into glass. Let stand for 10 minutes. Do drops rise to surface and gradually unite? Explain.

Pour the oil-in-detergent solution from (1B) into bottle. Shake vigorously. Then pour mixture back into glass. Let stand for 10 minutes. Are any oil drops visible inside of liquid? Any visible on the surface? Do they unite? Explain.

86

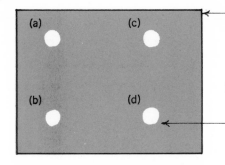

a clean plate of clear glass (or use surface of a pocket mirror) you **may** see tiny drop of oil surrounded by a dry film after the water evaporates

3. Testing for oil drops.

   Using a medicine dropper, take drops from the surface of each of the oil-water mixtures. Then take drops from interior of each mixture. Place drops on a clean plate of glass. Take samples where **no** oil is visible. Wait one half hour or longer for water to evaporate. If a tiny drop of oil remains on plate, what does it indicate?

cut gauze into two pieces 2" × 3"

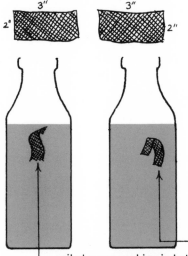

4. Test cleansing of strips of dusty, oily material (gauze).

   Rub each piece of gauze along floor or a dusty molding. Then add a few drops of oil to **each** piece, right over the dust particles.

soiled gauze soaking in hot water

soiled gauze soaking in hot water (containing dissolved **detergent**)

Fill two bottles with hot water and add detergent to **one**. Let each piece of gauze soak for 10 minutes, then do the following:

(a) Cover each bottle with hand and shake vigorously 15 times.

(b) Examine **surface** of liquid in each bottle. Any solid particles visible? Oil drops? Explain.

(c) Pour off liquid from each bottle. Then refill with warm water and rinse gauze pieces. Repeat 3 times with each bottle. Examine surface of the water of last rinse.

(d) Remove gauze strips. Squeeze out the water. Place strips on clean (dry) surface to dry out. Are there any differences in washing results? Explain.

FURTHER READING

When you consult some of the books listed below you will find that the same subject is often treated differently by different authors. This is all to the good, for varying points of view usually lead to a deeper understanding of a particular subject. Be sure to use the index of a textbook to find what you are seeking. Some books are more difficult than others. If you find one that is too simple, then go on to a more difficult book. You will learn more if you are not content with oversimplification. Finally, if the books listed are not available in your school or public library, any other recently published textbooks in physics or chemistry probably will serve you equally well.

Azimov, Isaac, *Understanding Physics*, vol. 1, Walker, 1966.

Boylan, Paul J., *Elements of Chemistry*, Allyn and Bacon, 1962. (Revised edition of book originally by Brownlee-Fuller-Hancock-Sohon-Whitsit.)

Gamow, George, and Cleveland, John M., *Physics: Foundation and Frontier*, Prentice-Hall, 1964

Metcalfe, H. Clark; Williams, John E., and Castka, Joseph F., *Modern Chemistry*, Holt, Rinehart and Winston, 1966.

Metcalfe, H. Clark; Williams, John E.; Trinklein, Frederick E., and Lefler, Ralph W., *Modern Physics*, Holt, Rinehart and Winston, 1968.

Miller, Franklin, Jr., *College Physics*, Harcourt, Brace and World, 1967.

Nussenbaum, Siegfried, *Organic Chemistry: Principles and Applications*, Allyn and Bacon, 1963.

Semat, Henry, *Fundamentals of Physics*, 4th ed., Holt, Rinehart and Winston, 1966.

Verweibe, F. L.; Van Hooft, G. E., and Suchy, R. R., *Physics — a Basic Science*, Van Nostrand, 1962.

Watt, George W.; Hatch, Lewis F., and Lagowski, J. J., *Chemistry*, Norton, 1964.

Weaver, Elbert C., and Foster, Laurence S., *Chemistry for Our Times*, McGraw-Hill, 1960.

White, Harvey E., *Modern College Physics*, Van Nostrand, 1966.

Many of the subjects treated in this book are thoroughly discussed in encyclopedias. It always helps to spend a little time consulting the index volume. You might try these:

Encyclopaedia Britannica, 1969.

Collier's Encyclopedia, 1968.

Compton's Pictured Encyclopedia and Fact Index, 1967.

The Encyclopedia Americana, 1970.

The Harper Encyclopedia of Science, 1963.

McGraw-Hill Encyclopedia of Science and Technology, 1960.

Van Nostrand's Scientific Encyclopedia, 1968.

GLOSSARY

ARCHIMEDES' PRINCIPLE — the buoyant force is equal to the weight of that body of fluid that the submerged body displaces; this statement holds true whether the submersion is partial or complete.

ATMOSPHERIC PRESSURE — the weight of a column of air 1 square inch in cross section and extending from sea level to the top of the atmosphere. Normal or standard atmospheric pressure is equivalent to 14.7 pounds per square inch.

BAROMETER — an instrument for measuring the pressure of the atmosphere.

BOILING POINT — the temperature at which the vapor pressure of a liquid is equal to the pressure on the liquid.

BUOYANCY — the lifting effect of a fluid upon a body wholly or partially immersed in it; it is also known as buoyant force.

CONDENSATION — the change from gaseous (vapor) state to liquid state; this change is accompanied by a considerable shrinkage in volume.

DETERGENTS — substances that are capable of dislodging, removing, and dispersing solid and liquid *soils* (grease-enclosed dirt and grime) from a surface being cleaned; soapless detergents are often called synthetic detergents or syndets.

DISTILLATION — the purification of a liquid or its separation from other liquids by vaporization and subsequent condensation.

EMULSION — a suspension of small globules of one liquid in a second liquid with which the first will not mix; salad dressing is an example of an emulsion.

EVAPORATION — the change from liquid state to gaseous (vapor) state.

FLUID — a general term denoting both liquids and gases.

FRACTIONAL DISTILLATION — a variation in the process of distillation used to separate a mixture of liquids with different boiling points into various fractions, or groups of liquids.

FRACTIONAL FREEZING — a method of purifying an impure liquid substance by cooling until part of it has crystallized; the remaining liquid containing most of the impurities is then poured off, leaving the purified crystals.

FREEZING POINT — the temperature at which a substance under normal atmospheric pressure changes from liquid to solid state; the freezing point and the melting point are identical for pure substances.

GRAVITY PRESSURE — the pressure exerted by a liquid due to the weight of the liquid itself.

PRESSURE — force applied to a surface, measured as force per unit area; it is expressed as pounds per square inch, pounds per square foot, a certain number of atmospheres, etc. (See ATMOSPHERIC PRESSURE)

REGELATION — the process of melting under pressure and refreezing as soon as the pressure is relieved; ice at the normal melting point, if subjected to great pressure, will become liquid and then "regelate" when the pressure is removed.

SIPHON — an instrument, usually in the form of a bent tube, for conveying a liquid over the edge of a vessel and delivering it at a lower level.

SOLUTE — a substance dissolved in a solvent; in the case of brine, for example, common salt is the solute, water the solvent, and brine the solution.

SOLUTION — a homogeneous mixture of solvent and solute; when water (solvent) and common salt (solute) are shaken together, brine (solution) is formed.

SPECIFIC GRAVITY — the ratio between the weight of a given volume of a substance and the weight of an equal volume of water.

SURFACE TENSION — the tendency of a liquid surface to act as if it has a thin elastic membrane stretched over it.

SURFACE-ACTIVE AGENTS — substances that have the property, generally, of lowering the surface tension of the solvents in which they dissolve; they also lower the interfacial tension between two immiscible liquids.

VACUUM — theoretically, a space devoid of air or any other matter; practically, a region of space in which the atmospheric pressure has been reduced as much as possible with existing pumping systems; *partial vacuum* is a loosely used term to describe a space in which the pressure is slightly below atmospheric pressure.

INDEX

The Author

HARRY SOOTIN has taught general science and physics in the New York City high schools for more than twenty-five years. A graduate of the City College of New York, Mr. Sootin began his career as a chemist and soon switched to teaching. He was a member of the faculty of the High School of Commerce in Manhattan and then taught at Flushing High School on Long Island. He has always favored the laboratory approach to science teaching, believing that it is most effective in interesting his students in scientific facts and ideas.

In addition to his teaching duties, Mr. Sootin has devoted much of his time to writing. He is the author of some eleven books for young people, including biographies of Isaac Newton, Michael Faraday, Gregor Mendel, and Robert Boyle. Mr. Sootin has written many science articles for magazines and for the *Book of Knowledge*. He is a member of the American Association for the Advancement of Science, the History of Science Society, and the Teachers' Guild.